Jennifer He

10/14/15

The
Anointing

The Gift,
the Grace,
the Power

The Anointing

The Gift,
the Grace,
the Power

DR. CYNTHIA JAMES

DEXTERITY
PUBLISHING

Unless otherwise indicated, Scriptures are taken from the *New King James Version.* Copyright © 1979, 1980, 1982, Thomas Nelson, Inc., Publishers. All rights reserved.

Scriptures noted AMP are taken from the *Amplified® Bible.* Copyright © 1954, 1962, 1965, 1987 by The Lockman Foundation. Used by permission.

Scriptures noted NIV from *The Holy Bible, New International Version®* NIV®. Copyright © 1973, 1978, 1984, 2011 by Biblica, Inc.™ Used by permission. All rights reserved worldwide.

Literary development and design: Koechel Peterson & Associates, Inc., Minneapolis, Minnesota.

Dexterity Publishing
P.O. Box 227357
Dallas, TX 75222

Printed in the United States of America

First Edition: April 2015
10 9 8 7 6 5 4 3 2 1

ISBN: 978-0-9908344-3-4

DEDICATION

I have many people to thank for their guidance and support after acknowledging the faithfulness of a God whose love remains unfathomable.

There is my pastor, and highly esteemed colleague, Bishop T. D. Jakes, at whose behest this project has moved from dialogue to a published work. I've never met a leader with such a profoundly generous heart for developing the skills and gifts of others. Additionally, those who saw to the execution and logistics, Zunoraine Holmes, Lance Wubbels, and Katie Washington.

Then there is the much needed encouragement and input of my spouse, Alvin James, and our adult children, who gladden our hearts by their confession of faith and scholarly attainments.

This book is specifically dedicated to my parents, Melvin and Thelma Rembert, who assured that I was introduced to Scripture at an early age.

CONTENTS

ABOUT THE AUTHOR

DR. CYNTHIA REMBERT JAMES is a psychologist and educator with two earned doctoral degrees and over fifteen years of experience as a graduate professor. Her credits include a career of three local pastorates in Northern California as well as national and regional positions responsible for leadership development and church health. Additionally, Cynthia James has served as Vice President of City Team Ministries, a leading missionary organization, training and sending missionaries to 96 countries. She is the recipient of numerous academic and civic awards for exceptional leadership, among which is the prestigious President's Volunteer Action Award.

In 2001, Dr. James was consecrated to episcopal office in recognition of long years of oversight to two western jurisdictions as Presiding Elder. After conducting evangelistic work in the following locations: Finland, Estonia, South Africa, several Caribbean islands, and Turkey, Dr. James was invited to join The Potter's House staff in 2012 in the position of Director of Christian Education. Dr. James has published numerous professional papers and two books, but takes immeasurable delight in her marriage of 46 years to Alvin James and the joys and challenges of having reared three adult children.

I BELIEVE THAT WHEN THE HOLY SPIRIT

is operating in and flowing through churches,

He will draw people.

YES, A SPIRIT-FILLED MAN OR WOMAN

OF GOD WILL DRAW PEOPLE.

He will

But more important than having a Spirit-filled pastor, which is very important, is having a Spirit-filled congregation, because the work of God is in the streets and not in the pews! It is not enough to hear an anointed soloist, or an anointed choir, or an anointed speaker or teacher. We need to move from being spectators to being participants in the raw infiltrating presence of God that He may indwell our lives in a substantial way.

T. D. JAKES

draw people.

INTRODUCTION

Jesus said to the servants,

"Fill the jars with water";

so they filled them to the brim. . . .

Then he called the bridegroom aside and said,

"Everyone brings out the choice wine first

and then the cheaper wine after the guests

have had too much to drink;

but you have saved the best till now."

JOHN 2:7–10 NIV

ou know the narrative. Jesus was a guest at a wedding in Cana of Galilee, and when the wine ran out, He honored the marriage by His first miracle and in the simplest and most natural way manifested His glory. He could have hyped it by making it theatrical and sensational, but that is not His style. Quietly with a word to the servants and using common water jars, our Lord and Creator did in a moment what He is ever doing, transforming an abundant supply of water into the gladdening juices of nature, "the best wine," but in this instance He simply did so without the vine and grapes. All of life is the domain of His kingdom, and there is no division of life that separates the sacred and secular in the sphere of His rule.

Just ordinary servants, not angels or prophets. Just earthen water jars, not golden chalices or silver goblets. Just a single unostentatious word of command, not a summons to kings and queens to gather and watch a mighty miracle performed in their presence. Just water from an ordinary well. Jesus' first miracle was such a beautiful integration of the supernatural with ordinary life, of the grand work of God who sweetens and increases our joys from less to more and more. His gifts become sweeter every day, and that is just the style of Jesus.

I love this story because it reflects what happens in our lives whenever Jesus is present. My best thoughts, my best self, and my best days are just jars of dull impotent water, but He hallows every corner of my life by His presence, and by His Word and power turns those into quality wine. All things done with the consciousness of His presence are sacred.

The manifest presence of Jesus Christ, or "the raw infiltrating presence of God" as Bishop Jakes has stated, is what I mean when I say that we need "the anointing" of God upon our lives. When I am talking broadly about the kingdom principles related to the anointing, I mean the gift, the grace, and the power of the Holy Spirit to change and influence every aspect of our lives.

What Is "The Anointing"?

Some people confuse the meaning of the anointing by using it interchangeably with one's natural gifts and skills or the spiritual gifts of the Holy Spirit or even what we study about the ways of God. While not meaning to minimize the importance of any of those, I want to emphasize that the anointing is the empowering and the enabling of the Holy Spirit; it is the same transforming experience that was given to the believers who were gathered in the Upper Room on the day of Pentecost in Acts 2. It was God taking the water of their lives—their natural gifts and the marvelous discipleship training of being with Jesus—and turning it into the best of wines, lives that made a difference in the first-century world, literally turning it upside down.

The anointing is what only God can do in our lives. It is what universities and ivy towers cannot do, what much learning between covers of books (which I treasure) cannot do, because the anointing comes directly from the mind, the heart, and the Word and the will of God. It is that additional gifting and endowment from the Lord that lifts us above the ordinary and causes people to wonder, *How did you get through that difficulty? How did your marriage hold together in that trial? How do you stand? How can you praise through it? How did you overcome disappointment? How can you surmount barriers and difficulties?* It is the water being turned to wine. It is the presence of Jesus.

The good news is that the anointing is not just for pastors or teachers or spiritual leaders. It is available to all believers. On the day of Pentecost, "They were all filled with the Holy Spirit" (Acts 2:4). We are *all* eligible. We don't have to be on a church stage to be anointed! We don't have to have an amazing voice to be anointed! We don't have to be able to play beautifully on an instrument to be anointed! But the beauty is that we can be anointed grandparents, anointed parents, anointed sisters, anointed brothers, anointed employees, anointed supervisors, and anointed entrepreneurs.

God wants us to realize that He has more for us than just dressing up and going to church. He has more for us than going through a routine and a form of religion. He wants us to have such a passion to get closer to Him that it penetrates deep into our bones. He wants His Word to become so alive in us that our study of it takes us deeper and deeper into an understanding of its revelations and riches.

When the anointing of God is upon us, we can't just settle for being church people; we want to be praying people who seek our Father's face. This goes far deeper and broader than we could ever go on our own. It is not denominational or geographical or philosophical, but the Spirit of God brings us to a place where we have such fellowship with Jesus that we become a mirror of His will and His character and His ways. We simply want more of Jesus in our lives—not the grandest car in the parking lot, not the biggest house on the block, not the finest suit or shoes or building to work in. We simply want to be more like Christ.

The manifest presence of Jesus Christ, or "the raw infiltrating presence of God" as Bishop Jakes has stated, is what I mean when I say that we need "the anointing" of God upon our lives.

It's All about Transformation

I believe you're reading this book because you feel drawn to pursue the anointing of God. I believe that you are among the precious group of believers

GOD HAS A WAY, A HISTORICALLY PROVEN WAY,

AN ANOINTED WAY, OF TAKING WHAT HAD

TO SEEM LIKE FAR DISTANT DREAMS

AND WONDERINGS OF THE 120 BELIEVERS WHO

GATHERED IN THE UPPER ROOM AND LIFTING

THEM ABOVE AND BEYOND THE ORDINARY.

of whom the prophet Daniel spoke these words: "The people who know their God shall be strong, and carry out great exploits" (Daniel 11:32). I am so delighted to declare to you that the Lord is not looking for your abilities. He's looking for your availability, and not for someone who is already perfect and has perfected every gift. He is looking for people who are willing to go and to grow and set themselves apart to follow Jesus.

Perhaps you feel like I did when I was in high school. No one ever suggested that I was "the most likely to succeed." I never drew anyone's attention that some day I might be likely to do anything significant. You may feel that there is no reason to think that you can rise to a higher level in life. But God has a way, a historically proven way, an anointed way, of taking what had to seem like far distant dreams and wonderings of the 120 believers who gathered in the Upper Room and lifting them above and beyond the ordinary. It was only a short time after their baptism with the Holy Spirit when the Jewish officials "saw the boldness of Peter and John, and perceived that they were uneducated and untrained men, they marveled. And they realized that they had been with Jesus" (Acts 4:13). How did they know that? Because despite whatever else they lacked, they were anointed by the Holy Spirit and brought with them the very presence of Jesus, and this made all the difference.

That amazing and unlikely transformation of what had been two frightened and hiding disciples into mighty preachers of the resurrected Jesus was not limited to Peter and John or the other 120 believers in the Upper Room. I've seen God do amazing things in countless lives, and in my own life as well. I was in my late twenties when I suffered a light stroke. At the time I was teaching at a university during the day and a community college at night as well as another job on the side—yes, I was pushing way too hard. One day after I came home from the university, I was so exhausted that I just lay down and went to sleep, and that night I had the stroke. Being so young, I was very frightened, and even more so when the doctor made the solemn pronouncement, "After nine days, Cynthia won't be able to lecture again. Her memory is not going to return. And she will not be able to drive." Initially, there was lingering weakness down one side of my body. But I want you to know that despite the prognosis and very real probabilities, God released an anointing upon me, restored me to health, and has opened doors of effective ministry that have been beyond anything I ever dreamed.

And the anointing can do the same for you. I believe the Lord is going to do something in your life even as you read these words. Seek Him like never before. When you turn the eyes of your heart and soul toward the Son of God, He can speak directly to your spirit and transform you into the person He wants to you to become. Tell the Lord you are seeking His gift, His grace, and His empowerment through the anointing. He will change your water to the best wine. He will pour out the anointing of His Spirit upon you that makes all of the difference.

The anointing comes directly from the mind, the heart, and the Word and the will of God. It is that additional gifting and endowment from the Lord that lifts us above the ordinary and causes people to wonder, How did you get through that difficulty? How did your marriage hold together in that trial? How do you stand? How can you praise through it? How did you overcome disappointment? How can you surmount barriers and difficulties? It is the water being turned to wine. It is the presence of Jesus.

THE SPIRIT-FILLED LIFE IS NOT A SPECIAL,

deluxe edition of Christianity.

IT IS PART AND PARCEL

...total

OF THE TOTAL PLAN OF GOD FOR HIS PEOPLE.

A. W. TOZER

plan of God...

CHAPTER ONE

THE SAME POWER THAT RAISED JESUS

"... how God anointed Jesus of Nazareth

with the Holy Spirit and with power,

who went about doing good and healing

all who were oppressed by the devil,

for God was with Him."

ACTS 10:38

am always amazed that so many believers who read that Jesus "often withdrew into the wilderness and prayed" (Luke 5:16) seldom find a quiet place and take the time to pray. How is it that Jesus, who is fully God in the flesh, often found that He must get away by Himself and spend time with His Father in prayer, and we think we don't need to do the same?

Now consider that Jesus, fully God and fully man, required the anointing of the Holy Spirit and with power. Jesus came forth from the seclusion of His life at Nazareth, where He had lived wholly within the will of God, and entered into His first public act through the baptism of John. "When He had been baptized, Jesus came up immediately from the water; and behold, the heavens were opened to Him, and He saw the Spirit of God descending like a dove and alighting upon Him. And suddenly a voice came from heaven, saying, 'This is My beloved Son, in whom I am well pleased'" (Matthew 3:16–17).

It was the anointing of the Holy Spirit at the launching of Jesus' ministry that made Him so effective and so successful, not His family name or His social status or His degrees and credentials, because He came from an obscure family. Once the anointing of the Spirit fell upon Jesus, His ministry exploded, indicating He is the Messiah, the Anointed One, and they began to call Him Jesus Christ. *Christ* is not His last name. *Christ* means "anointed" and is the Greek translation of the Hebrew word rendered Messiah. "Christ" is symbolic of the endowment of the Holy Spirit falling upon Him. It denotes that He was anointed or consecrated to His great redemptive work as Prophet, Priest, and King of the people. He is Jesus the Christ. That is why sometimes we hear Him called "Jesus Christ" and at other times we hear Him called "Christ Jesus."

If Jesus must be anointed with the Holy Spirit and power to fulfill His purpose for coming to the world, "doing good and healing all who were oppressed by the devil, for God was with Him," how much more do we need the same gift and enabling power? We need that extra, but it really isn't an extra; it should be essential, because it's a mandated experience to be impactful. To work on your job, to live in your house, to deal with the people you're dealing with, to live in a way that reflects God's glory, it takes an anointing from God. To be authentic Christians, to be real and not just a model or an attempt to look the part, requires that God pours out the anointing of the Lord upon us. When we open our hearts to be close to Him and to be His child, He sends His Spirit to abide in us and to empower our lives in ways that are discernible by those around us. They can tell it only comes from the Lord.

I love the scriptures that declare that the same power that raised Jesus from the grave will raise us. The apostle Paul stated, "And God both raised up the Lord and will also raise us up by His power" (1 Corinthians 6:14). If that was not clear enough, he adds, "But if the Spirit of Him who raised Jesus from the dead dwells in you, He who raised Christ from the dead will also give life to your mortal bodies through His Spirit who dwells in you" (Romans 8:11). Time has not depleted the supply of the Holy Spirit one iota—it is not relinquished, it is not dissipated, it has not disappeared. The same power, the same identical power, not a duplicate, not an imitation, not a derivative, but the same beyond measure power that raised Christ from the dead is the power that is not only going to raise us but that is quickening us and enabling us and giving us that extraordinary impact today!

KNOW THAT THERE WILL BE OPPOSITION

Immediately after Jesus was anointed with the Holy Spirit, we are told that "Jesus was led up by the Spirit into the wilderness to be tempted by the devil" (Matthew 4:1). I want you to know that when you begin to explore walking in the anointing of God, you need to brace yourself for new testings and trials. Whenever we dare to begin to seek what the Holy Spirit has been charged to do in our lives as believers, look for opposition. The enemy is not challenged by us just going to church and putting our name on the roll. But when we talk about the power of God and the Holy Spirit, we are rolling up our spiritual sleeves and going eyeball to eyeball with the enemy. We are going to be in opposition to the adversary.

In this regard, I love the prophetic words that Isaiah wrote: "It shall come to pass in that day that his burden [the Assyrians, who were the enemies of Israel] will be taken away from your shoulder, and his yoke [the work of the oppressor] from your neck, and the yoke will be destroyed because of the anointing oil" (Isaiah 10:27). In verse 16, Isaiah spoke about the people of Israel being "fat ones." When the Scriptures speak about how the Lord will make Israel fat, it is talking about the favor of God upon them and how the Lord will make Israel prosperous. We want to be fat, rich, and thick in the things of God.

Isaiah is saying that although your neck has increased, the enemy has designed and cut out a yoke and a burden that he has labeled with your name, and he will try to put it on you, because the Word of God has come into your life and you are walking and living in the Word of God and in the promises of God. You are expanding and increasing, living off the abundance of God's blessings and the mind of Christ.

There are things that only the Holy Spirit can speak into our lives, the deep things of God. Only He can sense and know and touch the needs and the cries of our inner spirit.

So the enemy wants to strap a yoke and burden around our necks. He will throw lies and doubts and questions our way. But we can say with biblical authority, "I'm not wearing that pettiness. I'm not wearing fear. I'm not wearing those negative thoughts. You can't snap that oppressive yoke on me." We can say that because we are told that the yoke will be destroyed because of the anointing oil, because "the blessing of the LORD makes one rich, and He adds no sorrow with it" (Proverbs 10:22). We can say, "I'm not wearing that. I have too much richness in the Word, too much abundance in Christ, and too much experience in the things of God."

We're not playing around when it comes to the anointing. We're seeking God and turning down our plate and turning over our cup so that we receive all that the anointing of God has for us.

LOOKING FOR CLARITY

I have a teenager in my house who believes that whatever one needs can be found through Google, and that Google has covered everything in the universe. While it is truly a remarkable resource, there are some things in our lives that Google doesn't know (no offense, Google). There are things that only the Holy Spirit can speak into our lives, the deep things of God. Only He can sense and know and touch the needs and the cries of our inner spirit. We must recognize that there are depths in our lives that only He can hold and comfort and heal and build up and mend. Only He can cause this spiritual part of our lives to grow and live and flourish.

In 1 Corinthians 14, the apostle Paul speaks about how the trumpets were used in ancient Israel to both rally the camps and rally the people together, to bring about a spirit of unity. The trumpet was blown in the wilderness to alert the people when they needed to journey and break camp, declaring, "Let's go with the move of God." The trumpet was also used when the warriors were told to prepare for war and be ready to go out against the enemy. Paul states that "if the trumpet makes an uncertain sound, who will prepare for battle?" (v. 8).

When it comes to the anointing, the importance of clarity and a certain discernible sound is emphasized by Paul, because we are listening for the voice of the Lord. Jesus said, "My sheep hear My voice, and I know them, and they follow Me" (John 10:27). We depend on the clear, discernible voice of God to give us direction, because without it we don't know what to do. If the sound is uncertain, it means confusion—in our lives, in our minds, in the body of Christ, and in the camp of the living God. We can't afford to have someone trying to interpret the Scripture by how they feel that day. We can't have a teacher mixing a little science, a little New Age, a little tradition, and a little Scripture. We need a certain sound. We need to hear the voice of God.

Sometimes there's a tremendous amount of noise and voices and calamity in our world today. We may be so distracted by it that we're taking our cues more from those around us than being able to hear the voice of God in our spirit. And if I'm looking at what my neighbor is doing and listening and following the sounds he or she is making, and I'm not hearing the certain sound from God, I'm in danger. I'm at risk. I might go to fight, but it might be the wrong enemy. I might retreat when it's time to engage. I might be ready to celebrate and be relaxed when the call is to go to spiritual warfare. Or I might be fighting when everyone else is praising the Lord. In order to be in sync, we want to get that closeness, to get our ears tuned. As we proceed, I'll talk more about how the anointing aids us in terms of our hearing God's voice.

The apostle John states that the key is the anointing: "As for you, the anointing you received from him remains in you, and you do not need anyone to teach you. But as his anointing teaches you about all things and as that anointing is real, not counterfeit—just as it has taught you, remain in him" (1 John 2:27 NIV). Now that does not mean we have a license to be unteachable. Clearly, we are instructed to be taught by pastors and teachers. But it is saying that in any area of our lives, any experience we need instruction for, the Holy Spirit is able to be a complete counselor, our instructor and teacher.

So we can't say, "Well, the Lord can't help me in this area." It keeps us from the excuses that "I didn't have a grandmother or father or someone else to teach me." Whatever we need, we can get from the power and the presence and the wisdom of God and the Word of God. His anointing teaches us about all things. When we are pressing, searching for an answer, looking for a solution, we don't have to feel desperate and desolate as though there is no help. The Holy Spirit teaches us.

When we are pressing,

searching for an answer,

looking for a solution, we don't

have to feel desperate and desolate

as though there is no help.

The Holy Spirit teaches us.

When we get that yearning and the passion for the things of God, the Holy Spirit is the best instructor, the best professor, the beyond professor. How does that work out practically in our daily walk? Well, sometimes the Lord will show you that you really don't need that thing you want so badly, or that He will provide a substitute for it. When you're in a difficult situation with your child, He may speak to your spirit and tell you what you need to say to get through to them, or perhaps He'll tell you to just smile and not say a word. He'll do that.

And that's why we seek the anointing. Not to be the most fabulous psalmist or the most fabulous teacher or whatever. That goes by the wayside so that Christ will be revealed and the love of God will be shared with the world that does not know that He has come to provide for us.

THE ANOINTING OIL ONLY COMES THROUGH CRUSHING AND BRUISING

I believe there's a special call from God to His church in our times. Every day the news—locally, nationally, and internationally—gets more devastating, and it's no longer just somewhere else where it is happening. We are impacted by the levels of violence and cruelty and unimaginable acts of inhumanity that occur all around us. The pressure of living in these days has the potential to be overwhelming.

Remember when Jesus was in the Garden of Gethsemane, facing the unthinkable pressure of the cross. *Gethsemane* means "oil press." It is the pressure that is put on the olive that brings out the oil. We are in the press of these very difficult times and days. Circumstances, a lack of justice often, a lack of fairness and prudence, are what bring out the flow, the anointing that God has made available to us.

One of the symbols of the Holy Spirit is oil, particularly olive oil and the olive branch. Why? Because the oil is secreted as the olive is bruised. The only way to get the oil out of the olive is to crush the olive. The oil costs the olive its life, its shape and form. The more we bruise and crush the olive, the more oil is secreted. The prophet Isaiah tells us that Jesus "was wounded for our transgressions, He was bruised for our iniquities; the chastisement of our peace was upon Him; and by His stripes we are healed" (Isaiah 53:5). Through

His bruising we become eligible to receive the oil of the Holy Spirit drop by drop, little by little.

In our own lives, the bruising we have received has brought us to a level of anointing that we could not obtain any other way. Paul said it this way, "If we endure, we shall also reign with Him" (2 Timothy 2:12). There is something about enduring and suffering that secretes an anointing that cannot be bought, cannot be bottled, cannot be captured—it comes through the bruising of life.

The word anointing is used in different forms in the Hebrew and in the New Testament as well, and it generally means to "pour on or to paint or to smear on or to rub in."

That bruising aspect is reflected in 1 John 2:19–20: "They went out from us, but they were not of us; for if they had been of us, they would have continued with us; but they went out that they might be made manifest, that none of them were of us. But you have an anointing from the Holy One, and you know all things." These were people who had left the believers to whom John was writing—the folks who had disappointed them and who didn't stay through the hard times. These are the people they expected to be there in their time of need. But the good thing is, according to John, that they were made manifest (it become obvious, clear, and apparent) that none of them were truly believers. So when the adversary whispered, "Let's have a pity party," they could say, "No, I'm going to shout for who left and what did not come my way, even though I thought they would stay and be permanent." That's a real victory when we can rejoice and say it became clear and now we know who is likeminded and who is like spirited because we can't tell on our own. It is "not by might nor by power, but by My Spirit, says the LORD of hosts" (Zechariah 4:6). Unless the Spirit gives us discernment, even when it comes through bruising, we will walk straight into danger and think that we've just made it to an oasis. "You have an anointing from the Holy One, and you know all things."

Later in this book we will study different aspects of the anointing oil and how each of those ingredients represents an aspect of the character of Christ, but I want to emphasize one major point here. As we go through the importance of the anointing oil, let's remember that because Christ is the head of the church and we are the body (Ephesians 5:23), the same anointing that flows on the head of Jesus is to be the anointing that flows down to us. Psalm 133 describes how the precious anointing oil on the head of the priest Aaron runs down his beard and to the edges of his garment, so it means we don't get oil that is a lesser grade than what is on the head. The same anointing and the same fragrance that it is upon Jesus is also upon us. Whatever the oil touches, whether a hand or a foot, the same fragrance and aroma and scent is released, and that's the fragrance of the Lord Jesus Christ.

I like to apply that principle of the oil to the tree described in Job 14:7–9: "For there is hope for a tree, if it is cut down, that it will sprout again, and that its tender shoots will not cease. Though its root may grow old in the earth, and its stump may die in the ground, yet at the scent of water it will bud and bring forth branches like a plant." We know that life will come at us and try to cut us down and destroy us. Because we have deep roots in God, there's something beneath the surface of our lives that we cannot see. When the wind blows and the top is blown off, it's our roots that will reach out and say, "God, give me a word. Touch me. Send Your Spirit to me. I'm looking for Him. If I just get a whiff that deliverance is over here, I'm going. If I sense that healing is over there, I'm going to send my roots out over there."

That's what happens with the people of God. Beneath the trouble and the bruising and all the pressures and disappointments that are visible, we have roots that are reaching out and extending and pulling in the fragrance and getting refreshment and nourishment from the Lord. So it's important that we get those roots in God. And the anointing helps us to do that.

DAVID'S PRIVATE ANOINTING

The word *anointing* is used in different forms in the Hebrew and in the New Testament as well, and it generally means to "pour on or to paint or to smear on or to rub in." For instance, when someone was going to become a king, there was an inauguration or coronation where that individual would be anointed for service. Some churches do something similar where individuals are anointed with oil and consecrated or set apart for the office or place of service that they have been called to in the church. The anointing was more than just visible oil being applied; it was about the inner working of the Lord in the person's life as well. So it is both symbolic and real.

In the Old Testament, David was first anointed as king by Samuel in the midst of his own family, then he was anointed as king over Judah, and later he was anointed as king over all Israel. David also walked in the office of a prophet (Acts 2:29–30), a king, and as the sweet psalmist of Israel (2 Samuel 23:1). David exemplifies in every way how the anointing is a pouring out of the Lord in our lives.

Take a few moments and read through 1 Samuel 16:1–13, where David was anointed by Samuel in the midst of his family. This is one story where it's important that you read for the tenor and to get the feel, the mood, the pattern of the text—not just the words, but read the Bible like Braille and get a feel for each word. Notice that when Samuel gathered the family of Jesse the Bethlehemite and his sons, Jesse did not even bother to have young David brought in from taking care of the sheep. Apparently all of the seven older sons were more impressive than David.

And notice as well that even the prophet Samuel fumbled around a bit when he was there to anoint the next king. He was ready to anoint Eliab, the oldest son who was tall and handsome, which would have been like anointing another Saul. But the Lord had to instruct Samuel that he was missing the mark: "Do not look at his appearance or at his physical stature, because I have refused him. For the LORD does not see as man sees; for man looks at the outward appearance, but the LORD looks at the heart" (1 Samuel 16:7).

Samuel was looking outwardly for the extraordinary, but God had chosen David, the eighth brother, who wasn't next in line or next, next in line, or even next, next, next in line. And the anointing does that. It is the expression of the sovereign grace of God that looks at the unlikely and sees true possibilities. Similarly, He brought Jacob and brought Joseph ahead of their older brothers for specific callings or purposes. And that's what God does. When He saw David, He said to Samuel, "Arise, anoint him; for this *is* the one!" (v. 13).

"Then Samuel took the horn of oil and anointed him in the midst of his brothers; and the Spirit of the LORD came upon David from that day forward" (v. 13). "In the midst of his brothers"—now this private anointing is pretty inauspicious and not very glamorous. People like to be anointed on the big stage, but to be anointed among your family suggests that before we're anointed in public we should be able to demonstrate and manifest an anointing among our brethren with whom we eat and work. Based on how big brother Eliab spoke to young David later when he showed up on the battlefield (1 Samuel 17:28), you realize that David had to take their little curt remarks and criticisms.

It would be years before David made it to the public stage, but from the moment of the anointing, the Spirit of the Lord came upon him. David returned to his shepherding duties, but if you fight the lion and the bear, as David did in preparation to face Goliath, it's good to have an anointing before you go up against a raw adversary. You need to know when you face the lion that it's more than just you in the battle. And so, the things of God and the anointing is precious and to be valued, treasured, protected, revered, and honored, whether you're working with sheep in the wilderness or great congregations in the heart of the city.

We are seeking the Lord for the private anointing, not just looking for the public stage. God is lasering in on our lives, as He did with David, and saying, "You're not next in line, but you're going to

No matter what dirt has been thrown on you, or whatever stone, whatever mountain, whatever obstacle, whatever hindrance, whatever barrier, whatever obstruction has been put in your way, God can raise you up.

be next. It's not your turn, but I'm going to put you up next." When the enemy tries to count us out, we can say it doesn't look likely, but that doesn't mean that God can't do it. Because as the Scripture tells us God is not a respecter of persons (Acts 10:34), the anointing is not a respecter of human systems and man's ordering and our counting and our discerning of how things should go and our proper methods.

I don't know about you, but that makes me thrilled! We can thank God for all that is coming into our lives that other people said would never happen. We can thank Him for all that He will do that is supposed to be past any kind of solution. Situations change, jail cells open, lions mouths are stopped, the pointing finger is put down, and God gets the glory and the victory. That's the kind of God whom we serve.

So What about You?

David's father did not consider him a candidate to be anointed by Samuel, and it is obvious that his brothers scorned him. So what about you? I want you to know that no matter what dirt has been thrown on you, or whatever stone, whatever mountain, whatever obstacle, whatever hindrance, whatever barrier, whatever obstruction has been put in your way, God can raise you up. The anointing of God is filled with the resurrection power of Jesus. It is for kingdom living that is still applicable today.

Jesus is raising us up. He said, "And I, if I am lifted up from the earth, will draw all peoples to Myself" (John 12:32). He is drawing us. He's saying, "Come on, I'm drawing you. I'm pulling you. Come to Me. Come and seek Me. Come search for Me, and you will find Me. Call upon Me, and I will pour out My anointing upon you."

He's drawing you at midnight. He's drawing you at three in the morning. He's drawing you at five in the afternoon. When you're driving down the road, He's drawing you into seasons of prayer, into new depths of faith and belief. He's drawing you out of doubt and fear. He's drawing you to new places of giftedness. He has new anointings, fresh oils, fine spices, precious oils that are straight from the heart of God. It's available for the people of God, and it's available right NOW.

So pray this prayer with me:

"Anoint me, Lord, for Your service. Anoint my mouth for Your witness. Anoint my ears to hear Your Word. Anoint my heart to embrace Your truth. Anoint my hands to serve You. Anoint my feet to walk Your walk. O God, pour out Your anointing, and let it flow like a river. Pour out Your anointing, and give me the same power that You gave to Jesus. Thank You for Your anointing, Lord!

"I receive Your grace and enabling power to become all You want me to be. No more almost getting there but not able to go over. No more about to go in but can't quite enter in. Unbelief and doubt may have stopped me in the past, fear may have come in and encroached as a trespasser in my soul, but it's going to be put out, kicked out, because I belong to the You. You are mine, and I am Yours. In Jesus' Name. Amen!"

If Jesus must be anointed with the Holy Spirit and power to fulfill His purpose for coming to the world, "doing good and healing all who were oppressed by the devil, for God was with Him," how much more do we need the same gift and enabling power?

WHEN THE SPIRIT OF GOD COMES INTO A MAN

with power so as to fill his soul,

HE BRINGS TO THE MAN'S SOUL A JOY,

A DELIGHT...

Be filled

an elevation of mind, a delightful and healthy excitement that

lift him up above the dull dead-level of ordinary life and cause

him to rejoice with joy unspeakable and full of glory. I commend

this exhilaration to you. It is a safe delight because it is holy

delight; a holy delight because it is the Holy Spirit that works in

you, and He makes you to delight in everything that is pleasing

to the Holy God. One no longer needs to seek another source

of excitement, for here is something more safe, more suitable,

more sacred, more ennobling: *"Be filled with the Spirit."*

CHARLES SPURGEON

with the Spirit

CHAPTER TWO

FRESH OIL

But my horn (emblem of excessive strength

and stately grace)

You have exalted like that of a wild ox;

I am anointed with fresh oil.

PSALM 92:10 AMP

hen we talk about the anointing, we're talking about the Holy Spirit's power to change, to make a difference, to transform our lives. And so the anointing is not a concept that ever grows old. It has not been ushered out. It has not moved off of the scene, but as it was for then, it is for now, and it is for the future. It's for every believer in Jesus, not just leaders and pastors and teachers. We all need the power of God.

You might think that for some positions in the church that it doesn't matter whether persons bring a spiritual anointing in addition to their natural skills, but is that really the case? If we're not careful today, we'll just figure, *Anyone can just slip into this office and this type of service*, but the body of Christ is not that way.

For instance, some years ago we had an anniversary service in the church in which I was serving, and for some reason the cameraman who was hired that day was someone from a local secular company. I'm sure that he was skilled and experienced, but it was obvious when we went to play back the video of the service that his interests were focused on what was of interest to him. With his primary focus on the attractive ladies who captured his eye here and there in the audience, he missed the essence of the service completely.

No matter what assignment we have, whether it's taking photos or serving lunch or preaching the sermon, we do it as unto the

Lord. It's not just about doing what's interesting to us, what looks attractive, or what looks like fun.

Anointed with Fresh Oil

In Psalm 92:10, David is praying and declaring to the Lord, "But my horn (emblem of excessive strength and stately grace) You have exalted like that of a wild ox; I am anointed with fresh oil." There is a perennial freshness in God. Each morning there is a fresh infilling of grace and strength through the Holy Spirit for the ministry and service of the day. Yesterday's leftovers will not suffice; each day must involve the fresh oil of anointing, a fresh expression, a fresh move of God.

David is stating that God has given great strength and great liberty and great ability and great empowerment like a wild ox. It is not brute strength, but it is excessive strength that is wed to a stately grace. We ought to make being empowered by the Lord attractive. It should be a draw to people. When people look at our lives as a man or woman of God, as a child of God, they look at how we handle the power. We're not wheeling it around and acting like generals. It is a stately grace that goes with the anointing, because it's not our anointing. It's God's anointing.

With the fresh oil of anointing, it's like there's something pushing me. There's a gear that's turning. There's something that's a promotion in my spirit. I'm not saying elevation, but that it is saying go forward with an unction. It's a hand, not on my back, but on my soul. A hand that's gripped my spirit and a voice that is saying, "Lean into the wind of God. Lean into the will of God." David was saying, "I've got all this penned up in me that God has given, but it's not just a wasted frustrating energy, because He's anointed me with fresh oil for the right now move of God, for what He is doing in this hour and in this instance. It's not self-manufactured, not self-appointed, but God has given it to me with a stately grace."

Whether it is on our job or in our home, when the anointing is flowing, we're not telling Him how to work. We're not giving God a prescription of how to move. So whatever He wants us to do, however He wants to use us, may He have His way. It takes grace and a spirit of obedience to learn how to move to whatever place God has for us. It might involve a redefinition on your job, or dealing with an aging issue, or facing a different pattern or a different configuration in your family. It requires that we put on the whole armor of God from head to toe. May He equip us, fix us, and deliver us with His stately grace.

Fresh Oil for Old Wineskins

The "fresh oil" also has another dynamic role in our lives as believers. Certainly if we've been involved in the church a long time, but even if only briefly, we must be careful, because we can become a little stiff and starchy and perhaps even legalistic and judgmental. We're at risk for that. We can just lock into our church routine and rhetoric and get stuck in a rut.

But remember that Jesus said, "Nor do they put new wine into old wineskins, or else the wineskins break, the wine is spilled, and the wineskins are ruined. But they put new wine into new wineskins, and both are preserved" (Matthew 9:17). Much like the life of a believer, the old wineskins can get bitter and leathery and brittle. But the new wine is still fermenting and the gases are expanding. There is growth going, because God is always moving. Our God is a God of expansion and growth and increase and prosperity and abundance. You can't put that in my stiff, starchy, legalistic, judgmental little mind and soul, because the old wineskin will burst. Right?

So what would they do with the new wine if they didn't have new wineskins? First, they would take the old wineskins and wash them in water to moisten them. Then they would rub or anoint the old wineskin with oil so it would become pliable and flexible again, allowing it to stretch and take new form.

That is precisely how the anointing keeps our lives fresh and relevant. The apostle Paul states that the Lord cleanses us "with the washing of water by the word" (Ephesians 5:26). We are washed in the Word of God, which brings freshness to my dryness, to my arid spirit, to my sense of heaviness and what would be oppressive and depressive. I submerge myself, immerse myself, similar to the idea of a baptism of our mind, in the water of the Word so that it can refresh me, and I don't have to be so easily cracked and brittle and broken and angry and mad and chipped out and fragmented.

How do I get this? Where do I find this? I enter daily into spiritual disciplines of prayer, of fasting and seeking God in worship, and in reading, in study, and in meditation of God's Word. It is developing a hunger for the things of God.

Then after we have been washed in His Word, we make ourselves available to be saturated with the oil of the Holy Spirit, with the flowing of God. The anointing means "to pour on, to paint on, to smear on, or to rub in" and to become internalized. It's not like a mask we put on and take off or a garment that we slip into and slip out of. It's not like a cologne or perfume spray or a dab or a spot of oil somewhere. But the Word of God gets embedded down in our soul so deeply that when people encounter us, they are not encountering us in our fleshly nature. They're seeing the Christ who has been rubbed in, so to speak: "It is no longer I who live, but Christ lives in me; and the *life* which I now live in the flesh I live by faith in the Son of God, who loved me and gave Himself for me" (Galatians 2:20).

David said, "I'm anointed with fresh oil." He is saying that through the anointing of the Holy Spirit, the life of Jesus that has been internalized is brought to the surface. So when people see you, they are seeing you and all of who you are in Christ.

Jesus added to the description when He said, "No one puts a piece of unshrunk cloth on an old garment; for the patch pulls away from the garment, and the tear is made worse" (Matthew 9:16). No one takes new cloth and tries to patch up where there's been a rent or a tear in old cloth, because the old threads are worn and not able to be strong enough to hold the integration of the new cloth. Take a moment and tell the Lord, "Thank You that when I am broken and brittle, You bring a new view, a new thought, a new oil, a new refreshing. Thank You, Jesus."

THE ANOINTING GIVES VISION

In Psalm 92, David goes on to tell us what the anointing with fresh oil does. He says, "My eye looks upon those who lie in wait for me" (v. 11 AMP). David is saying, "I can see those who are false around me and all of the deception coming my way, because I can see with a discerning eye. I see where the enemy has set up to trick me and trap me. I see where he has a design against me. When the enemy thinks that he is obscured and hidden, I can see him lying in wait like a crouching lion."

The anointing gives vision—a sense of what God's vision is for our lives. Proverbs 29:18 AMP states, "Where there is no vision [no redemptive revelation of God], the people perish." This happens when there's a lack of the ability to see. Through the anointing, I see my destiny and can establish the right goals to have that fulfilled. Because I can see, I am not living in confusion, and I am not giving in to hopelessness or depression, but I am living with purpose. Rather than perishing, I am flourishing like the palm tree and the cedar (Psalm 92:12). God has made provision for us that we can see and walk in our destiny.

The anointing is not a concept that ever grows old. It has not been ushered out. It has not moved off of the scene, but as it was for then, it is for now, and it is for the future.

The importance of having vision was demonstrated for us in the whole account where the prophet Samuel went to anoint one of the sons of Jesse as king (1 Samuel 16). Samuel thought it must be the oldest son in Jesse's house, Eliab, who looked the part. Samuel did not have the vision to see what God was doing, and so the Lord told him to stop looking on the outward appearance and to see what God looks at—the heart. So we can't trust what we see outside of the anointing. David's seven brothers looked good, walked good, talked good, promised a whole lot, but Samuel needed to see with the eyes of the spirit. The lesson about Samuel anointing David is to let us know the danger of seeing without the anointing.

In Habakkuk 2:2–3, the prophet tells us how important it is for us to have a vision: "Write the vision and make it plain on tablets, that he may run who reads it. . . . Though it tarries, wait for it; because it will surely come, it will not tarry." That means that we will never reach the potential of our dreams and what God has for us if we don't learn how to see. We don't have anything to write if we can't see. Thus the desire for us to have sight and to be able to see.

That same passage goes on to talk about the vision of what we see in God is for an appointed time. "For the vision is yet for an appointed time; but at the end it will speak, and it will not lie. Though it tarries, wait for it; because it will surely come, it will not tarry." That means it's worth waiting on God for whatever we have to go through to get a sense of what God has ordained for who we are, where we're going, what we're going to do, what we're going to conquer, and where He's going to take us. It can come as a thought or a conviction in our heart, but "wait on it, though it tarries." It may seem as though it's coming slow, but wait on it, because it will speak and it will not lie. It means that the anointing of God will testify on your behalf. What people thought came out of your flesh, out of your imagination or a whim, is not something you dreamed up, not something you asked to do, but it is the anointing you received from God.

This is why it is so important to get your spiritual sight. It's why a holy imagination is so important. It's why faith is so important in the people of God. Because if you can see it, you can say, "Okay, I know how to adjust. I can see where the Lord is trying to work this out. I can begin to see what God has promised He's going to deliver. He's going to make good on it. And I can walk in His plan for my life."

Revelation 3:18 says, "Anoint your eyes with eye salve, that you may see." When I was growing up, my mother had an ointment that she put on everything that went wrong. If I had a skinned knee, if I had a bump on my hairline, or if I broke a bone, she put that ointment on it. It was her mainstay. She put her confidence in it, whether it was actually effective or not. But we want to make sure that we understand that the Word of God can be applied to our vision as a salve, as an anointing that opens our eyes. Like the blind man in John 9 whom Jesus healed, we can say: "One thing I know: that though I was blind, now I see."

It is interesting that Psalm 92 is particularly a psalm of deliverance—a song that comes from the Author and the Finisher of our faith and makes its lyrics and melody in our hearts. It is the only psalm that is noted at the beginning as "a Song for the Sabbath Day." That does not mean that it was

EACH MORNING THERE IS A FRESH INFILLING

OF GRACE AND STRENGTH THROUGH THE

HOLY SPIRIT FOR THE MINISTRY AND SERVICE

OF THE DAY. YESTERDAY'S LEFTOVERS WILL

NOT SUFFICE; EACH DAY MUST INVOLVE

THE FRESH OIL OF ANOINTING, A FRESH

EXPRESSION, A FRESH MOVE OF GOD.

written exclusively for the Sabbath, but it does mean that this is a good psalm to use on the day of rest. Remember that throughout Scripture, the Sabbath day itself, the notion of Sabbath, and the notion of Jubilee were concepts of relieving burdens. The Sabbath was a concept of entering into rest, and faith, and belief. So this scripture is saying that I'm going to see God give new vision. I can't see it now. I'm looking as through a glass darkly. It's a smoky mirror, but after awhile He's going to open my eyes. So He's talking about deliverance coming. He's talking about opening. And the anointing brings the opening.

THE ANOINTING GIVES REVELATION

David continues in Psalm 92: "My ears hear my desire on the wicked who rise up against me" (v. 11). That sounds unbelievable. We really may not hear the words, but we can discern in our spirit there's plotting going on against us by the enemy. There's some conspiracy going on with the adversary whose desire is to steal, kill, and destroy. We can almost visualize the opposition or sense it in a spiritual way. And we can sometimes even anticipate what the enemy is going to send next.

It really is true. Try it. Seek the Lord, because the Scripture states it. "Surely the Lord GOD does nothing, unless He reveals His secret to His servants the prophets" (Amos 3:7). Before the Lord does a thing, He reveals it to the seekers of the Lord. You may say that you're not a prophet, but He gives us a sense of His movement. The Lord wants us to follow Him, and He's not playing games.

When the voice of the Lord speaks, it always lines up with the Word of God. Whereas Scripture speaks to us clearly and definitively, the enemy is vague and unclear, only brings confusion and leaves us perplexed, and never leads us into truth. God shares with us what His will is, and we rely on having a sense of His peace in us. We look for that, because when that peace is not there, we begin to say, "Have I missed God in some way?" So He does share and reveal to us.

David is saying, "My spiritual ears, since I have this anointing, can hear what the enemy is plotting against me. God is telling me, 'Don't go there. Stay home. Do this. Don't say that. Don't get in that argument. Don't get in that discussion.' My spiritual ears can hear. I won't be caught off guard. I won't be caught by surprise. I won't be caught in a place unsuspecting, because I can hear what others cannot hear."

There is a very instructive miracle in Mark 7:31–37 that regards the opening of our ears. But before I get to the story of the healing of the deaf-mute man, I want to note what is not so obvious at its inception. In v. 31, when Jesus left Tyre and went through Sidon and down to the Sea of Galilee, that was a totally circuitous route. Those who study the geography of the text are confused as to why Jesus would go this way, because it's not the straightway. I have found often that when there are patterns in Scripture, the patterns are repeated both in the environment and the typography of the land and the way things open up in the narrative. So consider here how the Lord doesn't always lead us directly from A to B to C in our lives. Sometimes He takes us the long way around for reasons He alone determines.

Much like the life of a believer, the old wineskins can get bitter and leathery and brittle.

Once Jesus arrived there, some people brought a man to Him who was deaf and had a speech impediment, which is not unusual for one who is hearing impaired, because we learn our speech largely from what we hear. Because of those impairments, the man was not in a position to present his own request in an ideal way. But there were people there who brought him and begged that Jesus would place His hand on him and heal him.

But rather than simply touch and heal the man, Jesus took more of a circuitous route. First, He took the man aside from the crowd, then consider what Jesus did—He put His fingers in the deaf man's ears. At best, we can only speculate as to the why of this method, but I think it was all about the personal nature of this healing, which is phenomenal. I'm so glad that the anointing is personal and comes directly from the Lord to us. Jesus is making it clear that the healing of our ears is going to come by means of who Jesus the Messiah is.

So Jesus makes a personal touch to the man's deaf ears, then "He spat and touched [the man's] tongue." Amazingly, we don't sense anything that is a drawback in this man. You get the feeling that the personal touch of Jesus overcame what otherwise might be considered offensive. We need to understand that to receive what we need from God to open us up, we have to be able to endure the things that would otherwise be offensive. There may be a stigma that comes along with being made alive in God, but I have to have what God is making available. Jesus is saying, "I will open your ears. I will give you speech. I will give you My word out of My mouth that will heal you."

At this point Jesus looks up to heaven with a deep sigh (v. 34), which is indicative of the communication between the Father and the Son. It's not a sigh of "Oh, I'm in trouble." This sigh is symbolic of the prayer. Whatever the nature of the communion, perhaps the relinquishing of the case to the Father, it is expressed through a deep sigh.

And Jesus gives a one-word prayer. Isn't it wonderful how God can work in an instant? He speaks in Aramaic to the peasants of Palestine and says, "Ephphatha." Just one word. Jesus can speak one word softly to you. He can whisper it to you, and you can feel the rumbling of all the earth and heaven. He speaks "Ephphatha," which means, "Be opened!" One word, and the man's ears were opened, his speech impediment was loosened, and he began to speak plainly.

This miracle is not typically considered as a passage about the anointing, but it's not distantly related because of having the spit on His finger and touching the man's tongue. There is that connection that is made, and it's not outside of the realm or feel of considering it with the anointing text of Psalm 92, where David says that through the anointing oil his spiritual ears are opened. He's speaking of deliverance in his ears. When this man's ears are open, he can speak right. Before, he could hardly talk.

Here is the point: It's dangerous to try to speak when you haven't heard. It's dangerous to try to talk when God hasn't spoken into you. So the man needed to have a touch, hearing first, because faith comes by hearing (Romans 10:17). He needed to hear so that he would be a right witness. Jesus told this man to not tell anybody, but the more he was told to be silent, the more he talked. How do you keep a healed deaf-mute person silent? It was magnificent evidence of what God through Jesus had done for him.

So know the connection. God through the anointing is getting His Word into our spirits so we can know God's voice and His speech pattern and His actual words. So when we hear or read something that sounds spiritual, we can discern in our spirit whether it is God's voice or not. We know His voice and His words, and then we can speak.

One last point from this miracle. Verse 37 states that the people "were overwhelmed beyond measure, saying, 'He has done all things well.'" This is connected to Genesis 1:31: "God saw everything that He had made, and indeed it was very good." They were pairing what God has said about His original creation, that it is very good. But it's saying more than that Jesus just did a great work. It's a statement, an evaluation by the subjects as it were, who paired it to God's original creation of man. It is saying to us that there is an aspect of the anointing that involves a new creation. It's not just pouring oil on my old rusty dusty frame. Ah, but when the power of the Holy Spirit comes into our lives, it is totally applicable and appropriate that they say, "This is beyond measure!" because the Holy Spirit has done a new thing, and it is as if there is a new creation.

BACK TO VISION

David said in Psalm 92 that the anointing with new oil was for the opening of one's eyes and ears. In Mark 7:31–37, we noted that just as Jesus' route to Decapolis was circuitous, so was the healing of the man who was a deaf-mute. Where Jesus could have simply spoken the word and healed him, He touched the man's ears and tongue and then He spoke a word of deliverance "Ephphatha." We saw how God's sovereignty and ways can't be charted or mapped out as to how He is going to move. We can't hook a GPS to God and say, "This is the route You must go." God may be leading us along a way that is unpredictable and unfamiliar, but He's going to get us there. Although we have the sense that we don't know exactly how and where, what it's going to look like, or what the scenery is going to be, still we will follow the Lord all the way to our anointing.

Now we come to the healing of the blind man in Mark 8:22–26. After taking a circuitous route, Jesus comes to Bethsaida where some people (in essence they were intercessors) brought Him a blind man and begged Him to heal the man. First, Jesus "took the blind man by the hand and led him out of the town." It is a beautiful time when God comes to us and takes us by our hand and spends time alone with us. I really love it when the Lord does His work in my life in complete privacy. Every now and then we just need to find a way to get alone with God. And He has a way of helping us to establish a prayer place, something that represents our prayer closet. It's a place, perhaps it's just sitting in your favorite chair or at your table, but you've designated a place and say this is one of the many places where I meet the Lord. We step out of life's activities and into His presence and soak in His Word. And while we're meeting with Him and being saturated in His Word, we're also asking God to make His anointing to be operative in our lives and to see victories.

Once Jesus and the blind man were alone, rather than just speak a word of healing, Jesus "spit on his eyes and put His hands on him" (see the circuitous route?) and then "He asked him if he saw anything. And he looked up and said, 'I see men like trees, walking.'" So there's another part to this deliverance. It's gradual; it's continual; it's a journey. "Then He put His hands on his eyes and made him look up. And he was restored and saw everyone clearly." So

God is telling me, "Don't go there. Stay home. Do this. Don't say that. Don't get in that argument. Don't get in that discussion." My spiritual ears can hear.

DISPLAY ONCE AGAIN HIS GLORY

TO A LOST WORLD.

DEL FEHSENFELD JR.

and empower...

CHAPTER THREE

WHAT THE ANOINTING DOES

The [uncompromisingly] righteous shall

flourish like the palm tree [be long-lived,

stately, upright, useful, and fruitful];

they shall grow like a cedar in Lebanon

[majestic, stable, durable,

and incorruptible].

PSALM 92:12 AMP

n the Introduction, I defined what I mean when I refer to "the anointing." Some people believe there is little or no difference between the anointing and the talents and abilities and propensities we are endowed with at birth. Others point to the spiritual gifts in the body of Christ as described in 1 Corinthians 12 and Romans 12. And there are those who speak even more specifically about a supernatural empowerment, an enablement, or an additional ability that may come upon a person for a particular assignment or task, which may only last for a season. I believe the anointing encompasses all of those various ways, which explains why the subject of the anointing can be a controversial one.

But while those are all important, I believe that the emphasis of the Old and New Testaments is that the anointing is primarily speaking about the empowering and enabling presence of the Lord. I'm trusting that as we walk through the Scriptures together, we will see and touch and be embraced by the living personage of Jesus the Anointed One, the Christ. I believe that whatever gifts we are born with, as well as whatever spiritual gifts we are given, come directly from the Lord. He has endowed us with these for His glory, for our good, and for the benefit of others, but we are being stirred and empowered for a greater experience of His presence.

Wherever we are in our spiritual walk, and whatever experience we've had in the Lord, I'm not trying to define what that experience will look like, what the giftedness will be, but I encourage you to open your heart during this season. There is a summons that is deep in the recesses of your soul. There is a beckoning in your heart that is saying to get on board with the Holy Spirit and allow Him to carry you to a new place. I invite you to shut yourself away with Him in a private place and seek His presence. It may be that you go there with rejoicing, or in repentance, or in service, or in sacrifice—but whatever your approach, go there. As I seek Him and make room for Him in my heart, I often find myself on my face, enveloped in His presence and embrace. It is His anointing, His presence that transforms me into the person He wants me to be. This is not an entitlement, but a true grace of the Lord Jesus Christ.

THE ANOINTING CAUSES US TO FLOURISH AND GROW STRONG

In the previous chapter, we saw how the anointing is symbolized in Scripture as fresh oil, which increases our spiritual vision and spiritual revelation. In Psalm 92, the psalmist wrote that because of the anointing he had been given God's vision for his life and acute hearing to know and understand the voice of the Lord. And we were reminded in the book of Isaiah that the anointing would destroy the yoke of the enemy. It said that the anointing so enriches and enlarges our lives in the things of God that the enemy's yoke will not fit on our neck. We are so fed and fat in the Word of God and the Spirit that the enemy cannot put on us anything that will entangle us. He can't hold us back or keep us under his control or bondage.

That same sentiment regarding what we receive in the anointing is beautifully expressed in Psalm 92:12 AMP: "The [uncompromisingly] righteous shall flourish like the palm tree [be long-lived, stately, upright, useful, and fruitful]; they shall grow like a cedar in Lebanon [majestic, stable, durable, and incorruptible]." Wow! Isn't that fantastic? Who wouldn't want their life to be described this way?

So who are the "righteous"? They are those who have the "fresh oil" upon them, who have the anointing of the Lord in their lives. They are in right standing with the Lord and His Word. They are said to "flourish like the palm tree." As tall as the palm tree is, the roots typically are only two- to three-feet deep and can search out water in desert places. This tells me that the anointing helps us to find refreshment. The apostle Peter, in his second sermon after receiving his own anointing of the Holy Spirit on the day of Pentecost, told his listeners to repent so "that times of refreshing (of recovering from the effects of heat, of reviving with fresh air) may come from the presence of the Lord" (Acts 3:19 AMP). The anointing of the Lord will help us find that kind of spiritual refreshing and reviving much like the provision of water in a desert place or in dry seasons. When we don't find anything working, when nothing seems to be coming through, and we're saying, "Lord, I just need a little drop. Just something to help me get to the next place," He will do that. He brings moisture to a dry and brittle spirit. He brings us refreshing nourishment and strength from the Word of God.

In Psalm 92:7, David had just said, "When the wicked spring up like grass, and when all workers of iniquity flourish, it is that they may be destroyed forever." What the psalmist is saying is that the wicked are also planted. They spring up and appear to flourish like grass, too, but it's short-lived. It's for a moment. It's but for a season, which David contrasts with the life of a believer. He says the righteous will flourish like the palm, which is long-lived, tall and stately. Why, asks David, would we get upset with what springs up overnight and is gone the next day, with what is here today and gone tomorrow? The anointed one is long-lived, stately, upright, useful, and fruitful. "The ungodly are not so, but are like the chaff which the wind drives away" (Psalm 1:4).

And "they shall grow like a cedar in Lebanon [majestic, stable, durable, and incorruptible]." The anointed life grows like the cedars, standing tall and

The emphasis of the Old and New Testaments is that the anointing is primarily speaking about the empowering and enabling presence of the Lord.

erect and endurable. Cedar is a hardwood that was used to build the palaces and the temples, but in addition to that it has a wonderful fragrance. And the cedar tree was used for healing, for leprosy. So he's saying that the believer is not like the grass that springs up and disappears, but we have a long life in the things of God. We're standing tall in the things of God. We're standing steadfast and unmovable. We're stable and set.

The cedar tree is said to have what some call "vegetative power." The cedar tree has a sort of plant intelligence assigned to it, obviously not a brain, but when the heavy snow is on the cedar, it has the ability to create a parasol, a pyramid. Its branches go up in a way so that the weight of the load does not easily break the branches. To make the connection to our lives, we know that when the weight is on, when challenges and difficulties seem overwhelming, we have a covering on us through the anointing. When the weight is on, we don't have to fall or break and come apart. The anointing is another voice on the inside. It's another encoding. It's an instinct like what is attributed to the cedar tree, so that when the pressure is on, it's highly resistant to anything that would harm us.

THE ANOINTING LEADS TO A FABULOUS LIFE

But that is not all that David says the anointing, "the fresh oil," does in our lives. In Psalm 92:13 AMP, he adds that the anointed one is "planted in the house of the Lord, they shall flourish in the courts of our God." So this anointing is not for us to go and declare, "I'm anointed," or "I have more anointing than you have," or "We have all of the anointing over here." No, the anointing leads us to be planted in the house of God. The anointing is meant for service. It's meant for worship. The anointing has a way of impacting and prescribing how I worship. Because I have been planted in the house of the Lord and in the courts of God, it is connected to my worship, which is reflected in the commitment that I make to God and the commitment that I make to church. So when you hear ministers and people say how the Lord sent them to this church, and then you can't find them two months later, you rightly ask, "I thought He sent you here? I thought you came to do this? I thought God spoke to you?" It's a lack of being planted in the house of God. The stability is missing in that person's commitment to God and to

THE ANOINTING OF THE LORD

WILL HELP US FIND THAT KIND OF SPIRITUAL

REFRESHING AND REVIVING MUCH LIKE

THE PROVISION OF WATER IN A

DESERT PLACE OR IN DRY SEASONS.

the people of God. The anointed one is not in and out the door. They are committed to being a part of the assembly of the body of Christ and to join with others in being in His presence.

David adds that the anointed one is "growing in grace" (v. 14). So we are planted, we are growing, and we are flourishing. "They shall bring forth fruit in old age; they shall be full of sap [of spiritual vitality]." He is saying that we go from glory to glory, from grace to grace, from faith to faith, empowered and energized by the Holy Spirit. Doesn't that stir up a new yearning within you for the anointing of the Lord? I believe this is going to create an appetite. David says that the anointing leads to being seasoned, always bearing fruit for His glory. It says a "[spiritual vitality] and [rich in the] verdure [of trust, love, and contentment]." We have the fragrance of the Lord. It's an exquisite place to be, like an exotic garden, abundantly green and tingling with spiritual life.

In verse 15, David states that the anointed ones "[are living memorials] to show that the Lord is upright and faithful to His promises; He is my Rock, and there is no unrighteousness in Him." We become a witness to the purity of God and the fact that He is always faithful to His promises. In other words, we are assigned to the world. God has placed His approval upon us and He has affirmed us as His servants, useful in the kingdom of God and doing the work of God, and it is a witness that our God has not forgotten about us. It's not always a word coming out of our mouth, but we are a living memorial, a living, breathing monument that shows that God is who He says He is. Our anointed lives demonstrate

We are a living, breathing monument that shows that God is who He says He is. Our anointed lives demonstrate that He is pure and undefiled, holy and perfect in all of His ways, and majestic and powerful.

that He is pure and undefiled, holy and perfect in all of His ways, and majestic and powerful.

How do I know God is powerful? Because we are still here. Because He is faithful to His promises and He is our Rock, the enemy has not taken us out. The Scripture says, "By this I know that the Lord loves me," because He has not allowed our enemies to triumph over us. He put a banner of love over our heads, invited us into the banqueting room, and spread a table before us (Song of Solomon 2:4).

This is what the anointing does in our lives, and David gets so excited in Psalm 92. He says we are living memorials to demonstrate who our God is. We become a banner. We become a walking sign. We become a neon light to show that the Lord is faithful to His promises. So when the victory comes, we can say, "The Lord did it. The Lord delivered me. The Lord healed me. The Lord made a way. The Lord kept me." People ask us, "How did you come through? How did you prosper? Why are you still standing? Why do you still have a sweetness in your nature?" And we answer, "Because we are living witnesses that God is faithful and His anointing is upon us."

People often say, "I'm not good at witnessing." But we don't have to be a professional in articulating our faith to others; we just have to be a believer and receive the anointing of the Holy Spirit. The fragrance of His presence will do its own testifying. The fragrance will announce itself. It's like when something good is baking in the kitchen on a rainy day. Those wonderful odors announce that something is coming. It announces that something has been blended and stirred and is coming forth to delight and sustain and comfort.

The Anointing Leads to Triumph through Suffering

In our lives, that fragrance from the anointing oil is not always what we think. It's not the promotion, or the name on the door, or the certificate, or the plaque we get, but sometimes it may be like the ingredient myrrh. In Exodus 30:23–24, God spoke to Moses and said regarding the making of the holy anointing oil for the tabernacle of meeting and the ark of the Testimony as well as to anoint Aaron and his sons as priests: "Also take for yourself quality spices—five hundred shekels of liquid myrrh, half as much sweet-smelling cinnamon (two hundred and fifty shekels), two hundred and fifty shekels of sweet-smelling cane, five hundred shekels of cassia, according to the shekel of the sanctuary, and a hin of olive oil."

Now remember, we are part of the priesthood of believers, and God is saying regarding our anointing, "One of the main ingredients that you must have in your life is myrrh." What is *myrrh*? It is the aromatic resin of a number of small, thorny tree species of the genus Commiphora that came to symbolize suffering. Interestingly, one of the gifts that the wise men brought to the baby Jesus was myrrh (Matthew 2:11). This means that the anointed one must learn to endure hardness, just as Jesus "learned obedience by the things which He suffered" (Hebrews 5:8).

How do you endure hardness? You get knocked down, and you get up again. You get bounced around, and you get up again. The Lord is going to allow some hardship and suffering to come into our lives. We may have to face the news that the X-rays haven't changed and the tumor is the same as it was weeks' ago, or that the corporate layoff includes us, or that our adult child does not want to hear a word about the faith.

One aspect of the anointing is that we learn how to endure hardness as a good soldier of Jesus Christ (2 Timothy 2:3). What does a good soldier do? A soldier keeps on going. A soldier keeps on advancing. A soldier keeps going forward. A soldier keeps on marching under the same flag, under the same banner, knowing that the Lord is our captain.

Many pastors seldom talk about suffering anymore. It's not a favorite topic to draw in big crowds. But the apostle Paul teaches us to rejoice over suffering, to rejoice over sacrifice. King David said to the Lord, "It is good for me that I have been afflicted, that I may learn Your statutes" (Psalm 119:71). If you've ever been through hard times, and I've had my share, you know that God was putting myrrh as a principal spice in your life! Nothing brings out the fragrance like actually going through it. Nothing has a fragrance like when you had to do without before you received it. The fragrance of the anointing oil is found in the fact that the Lord kept you when you couldn't make it. You didn't backslide when you didn't have the victory, when you didn't have the healing, when you didn't have the triumph. No, He kept you and brought you and led you and made a way for you as you went through it.

I want to focus on this because this is where our lives meet the real road of life. When we studied Mark 7 and 9, we saw that Jesus sometimes takes a circuitous route in our lives. He may bring us the long way around, but later we see it clearly. We can see in the distance what God is going to do. He's going to keep His promises. He's a faithful God. He's a mighty God. He's a wonder-working God who is worthy of all of our love and praise.

You woke up after the surgeon's knife. Praise God. You were able to make ends meet. Praise Him. You were able to work two and three jobs. Praise Him. You didn't deny Him. You didn't curse Him. But you said, "Bless the Lord, oh my soul, and all that is within me, bless His holy name. Bless the Lord, for He has done great things. Great things in my life!"

I want to come through life's difficulties and flourish, not fizzle.

Yes, the wise men brought the gold and the frankincense, but I'm declaring that they also brought the myrrh to Jesus. I will rejoice when the anointing has the fragrance of pain. I will be as a palm tree and a cedar and stand when the hurt, the rejection, the false accusations, and the abandonment come my way. I will flourish and grow in grace because I am planted in the house of my God, who is my Rock!

THE ANOINTING PUTS LIFE INTO FULL PERSPECTIVE

If you revisit Mark 7 and 9, you'll see that Jesus made it clear that He can take any route He wants to work in our lives. There's also another powerful lesson tucked in between the two healings we studied. In Mark 7:27–30, Jesus asked His disciples, "Who do men say I am?" They replied John the Baptist, or

Elijah, or one of the prophets. Then He asked, "But who do you say that I am?" Peter answered, "You are the Christ," the Messiah, the Anointed One. And yet when Jesus then explained that He must suffer and die and rise again, Peter actually rebuked Jesus, which earned Peter the same rebuke from Jesus that's given to demons when they began to announce that Jesus was the Messiah.

Why did Jesus do that? Because they knew who He was, but they didn't understand the full picture. Because if we think Jesus is only the deliverer, only the blesser, only the lover and keeper of our souls, we're completely wrong. Neither the demons nor Peter really had a right to confess Him, even though they were correct, because they didn't have the revelation of what the full anointing meant.

So Jesus turned Peter's statement that He was the Anointed One and gave some clear instructions: "Let me tell you about the Son of Man. He must suffer many things." He began to teach His disciples on suffering, and you need to know that an anointed life will bring you some suffering. But the anointing is so worth it! We need the lessons out of it. We need to get the anointing so we can get the instructions out of it. I want to come through life's difficulties and flourish, not fizzle. I want my God to take the grace and the strength and the abundance of life and blessing He has put on the inside of my life and make me a living memorial for others to see what kind of God and Father He really is!

I trust that you want the same. It's all wrapped up and can only be found in the anointing.

Myrrh is the aromatic resin of a number of small, thorny tree species of the genus Commiphora that came to symbolize suffering in the holy anointing oil.

The anointing makes things easy. not fatigued It is either there or not. Work up Just and fair

THE WORLD HAS YET TO SEE WHAT GOD CAN DO

with and for and through

AND IN A MAN OR WOMAN

WHO IS FULLY ANI

...see what

WHOLLY CONSECRATED TO HIM.

HENRY VARLEY

God can do...

CHAPTER FOUR

THE ANOINTING REQUIRES OBEDIENCE

"Has the LORD as great delight

in burnt offerings and sacrifices,

as in obeying the voice of the LORD?"

1 SAMUEL 15:22

his may sound very basic, but in order to receive the anointing of the Holy Spirit, we must have the faith that God is who He says He is, "for he who comes to God must believe that He is, and that He is a rewarder of those who diligently seek Him" (Hebrews 11:6). We must have the faith that God has grace to solve our problems, to give us solutions to the questions that are in our minds. We have to believe that the anointing is given of God, and it is given as a gift of His grace for us personally.

In order to have that faith, we have to resist doubt and unbelief, which are not the same things. Doubt does not believe what God has said, because doubt doesn't know what God has said. Doubt doesn't know that God has made His anointing available to us, so in doubt we do not believe God for it. But unbelief knows what God has said and refuses to believe and receive what God has said. So unbelief will hinder us from entering into the manifest presence of God.

That is made clear in Hebrews 3:12, 19, where it describes how the people of Israel were prevented from entering into what God had for them in the Promised Land because of "an evil heart of unbelief." They knew what God had said, knew that God is true, had experienced the presence of the Lord, and had heard the voice of the Lord, but it just didn't fit their agenda at that moment. Theirs was an intentional, deliberate refusal to respond to the

Doubt does not believe what God has said, because doubt doesn't know what God has said. Unbelief knows what God has said and refuses to believe and receive what God has said.

invitation of God, and we are warned through their example to not do the same.

So unbelief can hinder the free flowing and the moving of the anointing and prevent us from fully implementing and exercising the giftedness and the assignments that God has put in our lives. By faith, we must say and confess what God has said. We must say, "That is what I believe. That is what's going to happen. My God has said He will make a way, so I'm looking for the way to be made. He has promised the anointing, and I'm going to walk in it. Because He has stated that He is the healer of my diseases, I'm expecting deliverance and healing. I'm looking for it."

We must actively promulgate and preach and teach to ourselves and witness to others that God has provided grace for everything that is in front of us as a barrier and an obstacle. Doubt must go; but even more than doubt, unbelief must go. So if we are hesitant about the anointing, the Lord has shown us, "This is for you." We cannot be hesitant to step into it for fear that if we go out on a limb that we will be hurt or disappointed or taken advantage of. If I know what God has said, and I still refuse to respond to it, I am in danger of falling into unbelief. All of these are related. Unbelief ushers in stubbornness and rebellion, which are often the result of pride and arrogance.

THE ANOINTING UPON KING SAUL

In the story told in 1 Samuel 15, it's during a time of war and conflict between Israel and the nation of Amalekites. The prophet Samuel told Saul, "The LORD sent me to anoint you king over His people, over Israel" (v. 1). Clearly, this scripture tells us that

Saul's anointing came from the Lord, not Samuel. If you read 1 Samuel 10, Samuel not only anointed Saul with oil to be king but it states that "the Spirit of God came upon him" at that time (v. 10). The anointing upon our lives does not come from our human affiliations—our licenses or ordinations or denominations. It does not come from our praying grandma and believing granddaddy. The anointing comes from the Lord.

The anointing is an outpouring of the divine that was upon Jesus (Acts 10:38) and is represented in the Old Testament priesthood by the anointing oil upon Aaron that flowed from his head to the hem of his garment. It is personal, in that God has given a portion of His power to us. Romans 12:3 states that to every person there is given "a measure of faith," which is not just positive thinking, but there's given to us a measure of ability to do and to see it come into performance. It is not just the promise of the Spirit but the substance to see it materialize.

What we are seeking is to know the Lord's power in greater measure. We want to know God in greater measure. Whether we have been seeking His presence for decades or just a day or two, we want a greater measure. I want to say it until it's fully transferred in my spirit. I want to say I want God in a greater measure until the angels begin to whisper it around the throne of glory. I want a bigger cup. I want a greater container. I want a greater capacity. I want a fuller knowing. I want a greater acquaintance. I want more of the knowledge. I want a bigger fellowship with God.

My soul is hungry for the anointing—not because it is not being fed, but the more I'm fed, the more I need and want. The more I know the Lord, the more I desire to know Him. The more I love Him, the more I know that He loves me, and I'm drawn deeper to Him. I come with my heart wide open. I come saying, "God, not only must I hear You, but Your presence must touch me. You must walk with me. You must open my eyes and open my ears and touch my heart. I need You to wash and purge me and fill me and soak me in Your Word."

OBEDIENCE CANNOT BE PARTIAL

Samuel came to Saul, who had been anointed to be the first king of Israel, with the instruction that he must "heed the words of the LORD." When

Israel was coming out of Egypt, the Amalekites had ambushed them and were enemies of war. The Lord told King Saul to go and literally destroy all the Amalekites and their animals. Today, we may not understand what it meant to live in that violent age or the level of evil within those societies, but consider the level of barbarity and murderous evil in parts of the world today and perhaps that will give some perspective.

What this says to me is that God is requiring that I would forsake my old sinful ways and my fleshly carnal ways, that I would put all of that to death, and that I would follow Him. That I would destroy the idols in my life and the wrong things I set my affections upon, and I would set my affections in God alone. We may not have physical idols, but sometimes we think a certain relationship or a degree or a career or some entertainment will satisfy the deep longings of our soul. But the answer is in Jesus alone. Everything else has to be removed and destroyed.

While judgment was coming to the Amalekites, another people group who lived among them, the Kenites, were warned to come out from the Amalekites so their lives would be spared, because they had been good to the Israelites. That warns us that we can't hang around people who are dedicated and headed for destruction. That judgment doesn't have our name on it, so we need to move out of the way. The apostle Paul warned, "Do not be deceived: 'Evil company corrupts good habits'" (1 Corinthians 15:33). There are some things that we should not go through, and we need to get off the path that's going that way.

So the Lord gave King Saul the clear order to utterly destroy the Amalekites, but he "and the people" spared Agag, the king of the Amalekites, and the best of the sheep and oxen. He and the people altered the instructions and made compromises for what they wanted. Unfortunately, this sounds like what we do all too often in our own lives. All the things we don't want, we get rid of, but we cling to the things we want, even when we know the Lord has said they must go.

TODAY'S ANOINTING VERSUS YESTERDAY'S ANOINTING

Rightly so, the prophet Samuel was grieved and angry with Saul, and he cried to the Lord all night (v. 11). Saul had been God's choice. He was anointed for the position of king and the Spirit had come upon him, but unbelief, stubbornness, and rebellion took his current anointing and shifted him into a yesterday's anointing. Samuel represents today's anointing. He is hearing from the Lord for what decisions needed to be done now. So today's anointing is having to speak the now word of the Lord to the man who has become yesterday's anointing.

When Samuel goes to meet Saul in the morning, he is told that Saul has moved and has already set up a monument for himself of his victory! He has so missed God's voice and gone his own way that he's made a monument to his own name. He's totally preoccupied with getting his credit, his reputation, his image established. Saul has turned aside from the place he supposed to be and is engaged now in an assignment that was not given to him.

When today's anointed one, Samuel, confronts Saul with the word of the Lord, Saul immediately declares that he has performed the Lord's commandment, but the key word in the chapter is the word *hear*. "But Samuel said, 'What then is this bleating of the sheep . . . which I *hear*?" In the Hebrew, to *hear* meant "to do." In Israel, to "*Hear* the word of the LORD" meant "to do the word of the LORD." If you didn't do it, you didn't hear. Samuel was saying to Saul, "If you performed what you heard, why do I hear sheep bleating?"

Of course, Saul tried to put the blame on "the people," and he even tried to put a spiritual spin on the sheep and oxen—that they were spared to sacrifice to the Lord! But Saul is speaking the words of the enemy, and Samuel ordered Saul, "Be quiet!" It's similar to in our own lives—sometimes you just

My soul is hungry for the anointing—not because it is not being fed, but the more I'm fed, the more I need and want. The more I know the Lord, the more I desire to know Him.

IF WE ARE HONEST PEOPLE,

WE RECOGNIZE THAT WE COULD NEVER

DESERVE WHAT GOD HAS DONE FOR US.

WE DIDN'T EARN OR MERIT IT.

IF NO ONE ELSE KNOWS, WE KNOW.

WE KNOW WHO WE REALLY ARE.

have to tell the devil, "Stop! That's enough. No more. Don't bring anymore defeat or doubt to me. I'm not going to remain sick. I'm not going to remain down. I'm not going to remain in adversity."

Samuel was delivering the right now word of the Lord and was not allowing any interruptions. The Lord reminded Saul that before he had a crown, before he had a throne, before he thought he had a kingdom with a big name and deserved a monument, when he was a nobody and he knew he was a nobody, it was the Lord who anointed him to be head of the tribes of Israel. If we are honest people, we recognize that we could never deserve what God has done for us. We didn't earn or merit it. If no one else knows, we know. We know who we really are. We know what we're fighting in our flesh. We know it's not about us or for building ourselves monuments.

In verse 19, I love the active verb in how Samuel asks Saul, "How did you *swoop* down on the spoil and do evil . . .?" One translation says, "You did fly after the spoil." Saul was told to swoop down on the enemy, but he rather swooped down on the material things. If we would go after God the way we know how to go after stuff we want, what a difference it would make!

So now Saul was trapped. He was exposed. He mixed obedience and disobedience, and yet he claimed, "I have obeyed" but the people took the spoil to "your God" (v. 21). He's telling Samuel that "you ought to be happy because I'm doing what you want me to do for 'your God.'" How quickly he's lost his relationship to the Lord.

Never Step Out of Your Anointing

First Samuel 15:22 is the key verse as to whether it is reasonable to substitute something, perhaps even a sacrifice to God, for obeying what God has said. Samuel said, "Has the LORD as great delight in burnt offerings and sacrifices, as in obeying the voice of the LORD?" Absolutely not. God wants us to be His and to belong to Him alone. The enemy would love to confuse us and make us think that because we do something, God has been satisfied. "Behold, to obey is better than sacrifice." It's better to hear what God has said and to obey than to give Him offerings.

This is a serious word, for Saul and for us. "For rebellion is as the sin of witchcraft" (v. 23). If someone accused us of witchcraft, we would be indignant. But it's saying that to rebel against God is to take what God has said and repackage it to make it fit our lifestyle, to make it comfortable and convenient, and perhaps even make it so we benefit from it. To do that is as serious and dangerous an offense as the sin of witchcraft. Samuel adds that "stubbornness is as iniquity and idolatry." It is not just some small time grievous act, because Saul had rejected the word of the Lord.

For that reason, God rejected Saul from being king. Then the truth finally came out. Saul admitted that he had sinned "because I feared the people and obeyed their voice." He didn't want to be unpopular. Very often people reject the things of God because they don't want to be rejected by people. What comes through the text is that when one may be fearful of rejection of people, it is much worse to be rejected by the Lord.

Everything started to unravel for Saul previous to this rebellion, when he was supposed to wait for Samuel to come and give a sacrifice offering (1 Samuel 13). It appeared that Samuel was late, and when the people began to scatter from his army, Saul stepped out of his anointed role as king and stepped into the role as priest and gave the sacrificial offering. This shows how important it is to know what we are anointed to do. He decided that because the anointed priest was not there, he could do it. He could put the meat on the fire and offer up the sacrifice.

On that occasion when Saul stepped out of his anointing, the dynasty was snatched from him and given to David's house, which was to become a kingdom forever. In other words, the Messiah came through the line of David because Saul lost the dynasty when he stepped out of the anointing. When we step out of our anointing, it not only has consequences for us but for our children and children's children. And I'm not just speaking about our bloodline, but for all of the generations that are somehow going to observe and be beneficiaries of our life and witness.

Saul lost both the dynasty and the anointing for his kingship, which was dramatically demonstrated when Samuel turned to go away and Saul seized the edge of Samuel's robe, and it tore (v. 27). When Saul reached for the priest's garment, remember it was anointed. Sometimes we can actually be tearing at another person's anointing, which is not meant for us. It's not given to us. And so Saul lays hold on someone else's ministry, someone else's anointed garment, because he has missed out in his own walk with the Lord. We must be careful, because we don't want to be the one who is tearing at someone else's anointing or to let someone tear at ours. The anointing that God has given you, the assignment for your life, may be a business God has entrusted to you, and you can make that business go and multiply like no one else. But you have to protect it and watch out from those who would be trespassers in the anointing that God has given you. There are violators and poachers who infiltrate the area, set up camp like nomads, and try to get free room and board in a place where God has given you a charge.

THE LORD WILL NOT SPARE OUR FEELINGS

Saul is given a right now word and told that the Lord has given the kingdom to a neighbor of his, who is better than him, referring to David. When God talks to you, He does not worry about your feelings. He gives you the truth straight on. Not only will Saul lose the dynasty and the kingship, but he's going to watch it go to someone he knows. There is nothing worse than having God give you an assignment, and you don't follow through in total obedience, only to have to watch somebody else do what God told you to do. It hurts.

I know something about this. Many years ago, I was going to speak at a women's conference, and I couldn't wait to give them my message. Truthfully, while I hadn't disobeyed, I was feeling too lifted up about the lesson, as though I had gotten the lesson on my own. When I got to the retreat, the speaker before me was a pastor's wife, a wonderful Christian who came from a very rough background. She probably didn't have any biblical training, her grammar was poor, and her delivery was not so good. But she gave the lesson I was prepared to give next, almost paragraph for paragraph. The revelation was there, the insight was there, the examples were better, and I could not believe this was happening to me. I had been too impressed with myself, and the Lord taught me that if my spirit is not right, He doesn't need me as His messenger. When she finished, everyone there was deeply moved by the Word. Then they called me to the podium, announcing the universities I had attended and the awards I had received. I got up and simply said, "Everything I was going to say was just said, and I have nothing to add to it."

Then I just humbly took my seat. The Lord did not spare my feelings. I was so embarrassed.

So here the kingdom was torn from Saul and given to David. And the Lord will do that. He'll skip right over us just as easy. The Lord says, "You don't want to obey Me? Here's somebody who will. And you're going to watch it happen."

Then He adds, "And also the strength of Israel will not lie or relent" (v. 29). One of the key things about the word *strength* is that it is a way of referring to the Lord, and this is a reference to the anointing of the Lord. The strength of Israel is the coming Messiah, the Anointed One—the empowerment, the strength, the enablement, the strength of One who brings victory to Israel. And this word *strength* not only means "victory" but also "enduring," like a brilliant light toward which one moves and advances. It stays there. It has an eternal brightness. So it is the bright light of Israel, the Anointed One, who is waiting on the horizon in the Old Testament. They only saw through a glass darkly, saw only in shadows, but the substance was there. And Israel was moving toward that bright light, toward the fullness of what God is doing in the day.

But despite Saul's failure, there is still unfinished business for Samuel. Agag, the king of the Amalekites, thinks he has gotten a free pass, but when the enemy has to go, he's going to go. Saul did not obey the voice of the Lord, but Samuel did, destroying what the Lord had said needed to be destroyed.

No Compromise for the Anointing

This story that regards the anointing of Saul gives us a chance to be honest and vulnerable. It

When God talks to you, He does not worry about your feelings. He gives you the truth straight on.

gives us an opportunity, while there's grace, to examine our lives and ask, what has God said that we have compromised? Did He tell us to do a mission work, and we just did one good deed? Or did He tell us to give away something, and we gave a portion of it? Did He tell us to forgive someone, but we decided we won't forgive them but we'll just try to get along with them? What has the voice of the Lord said to us that perhaps we have reformed and repackaged? What have we not done or what have we kept? Is there an ounce anywhere of resistance? Of stubbornness? Have we tried to paint over what the Lord has said?

Yes, we absolutely should became enthralled with the concept of the anointing and remember how it glorifies Christ and how we are made to be powerful witnesses. But along with that, we must make certain that hindrances to the anointing are removed. While most of us know that sinful pleasures must be dealt with, this issue of resistance can be so subtle. Is there just a thin layer of pretense anywhere?

If so, let us repent and return to the anointing of the Holy Spirit. We're not perfect people, and God is not looking for perfect people. He said what He's looking for is available people and willing hearts. That is where His presence and anointing abides!

What has the voice of the Lord said to us
that perhaps we have reformed and repackaged?
What have we not done or what have we kept?
Have we tried to paint over what the Lord has said?

SPIRIT-FILLED SOULS ARE ABLAZE FOR GOD.

THEY LOVE WITH A LOVE

that glows.

THEY SERVE WITH A FAITH

that kindles.

THEY SERVE WITH A DEVOTION

that consumes.

They rejoice with

THEY HATE SIN WITH FIERCENESS

that burns.

THEY REJOICE WITH A JOY

that radiates.

LOVE IS PERFECTED IN THE FIRE OF GOD.

SAMUEL CHADWICK

CHAPTER FIVE

Longing for the Anointing

As the deer pants for the water brooks,

so pants my soul for You, O God.

My soul thirsts for God,

for the living God.

Psalm 42:1–2

hile the story of King Saul vividly teaches us about those aspects of our lives that hinder the flow of the anointing and God's presence and power in our lives, it is vital that we move on and focus our attention on the positives that draw us into and a longing for the anointing of the Holy Spirit. This is a serious endeavor that we're on, and I recognize that when we talk about the presence of the Lord in our lives and how God calls us and sets us aside for service, it can be somewhat of an elusive subject.

I firmly believe that if we align our lives with the principles of the Word of God, we will find that the draw and the attraction to those things that hinder the flow of the anointing will be minimized and removed in our lives. My purpose in this chapter is to highlight several scriptures that, if we embrace them in our lives, encourage us to seek the move of God. Remember that when I refer to the anointing, I mean the presence of Jesus in our lives.

WHEN OUR SOUL THIRSTS FOR GOD

In Psalm 63, David was in the wilderness of Judah, and from that wild, barren region his prayer begins: "O God, You are my God; early will I seek You." When he declares, "O God, You are my God," he was not referring to God as some ideological form, some distant concept, or some figment of his heritage. No, David was saying, "God, You are real, and You're right here with me. You are my God. You made me. You created me. You're the one true God to whom I am looking. You're the one to whom I'm turning. I'm not running here and there, but I am looking to You alone."

Then David gives us a sense of his passion and longing for the presence and the anointing of God when he cries, "Early will I seek You." I don't think David was merely talking about the early morning hours, but he was saying, "Wherever I am, I want to meet You at the start of everything in my day. I want to be with You at the beginning of my decisions. I want my journey to be launched from where You are, God. You are my first and only priority, and I am asking You to come to me. I know that You are present everywhere, but it is Your tangible presence that I seek, when Your invisible presence is almost on the brink of being visible, when Your presence so saturates the atmosphere around me that it's as if I can touch and feel Your presence!"

I translate David's desire to see God into my own life by praying, "God, before I make this step, before I speak this word, before I make this decision, before I receive this opportunity, before I walk through this door, I want to lay my heart before You and hear from You first. Early will I seek You. I'm inviting You in this season to alter my schedule, to set a prayer time in my life, for I must meet with You, and I surely must hear from You, O God. I want You to adjust the dial of my spirit. I want You to tune me in to You. I'm looking for You."

David continues his prayer: "My soul thirsts for You." In other words, "My soul is dry for You, O God. My soul desperately needs watering. I need a different thought than what I can manufacture. I need different feelings and opinions that don't emanate out of my own experience. My soul is thirsty for You." Then David adds, "My flesh, even my flesh, longs for You. Every part of my being is longing and looking for You, the living God." And he says, "I'm in this dry and thirst land where there is no water." How sad and weary our life is without the presence of God. There is no life-sustaining water there.

"So I have looked for You in the sanctuary, to see Your power and Your glory." In other words, "I've come for You in the place where there is faith. I've connected with the congregation of believers. I'm looking for You, O God. I'm looking for You in the songs and the prayers, in the people of God, in the praise of Your great Name. I am desperate to see Your power and Your glory."

David's prayer is vibrating with intensity for how much he desires the presence of the Lord. We know how good it feels when someone truly loves and wants us and how we are drawn to them. This is what David is drawn toward in the anointing. "God, I'm waiting for You. I'm looking for You everywhere. There is nothing I desire more than You. I long for Your presence."

And David was hardly alone in this passionate pursuit of God. The prophet Isaiah said, "With my soul I have desired You in the night, yes, by my spirit within me I will seek You early" (Isaiah 26:9). Take these words of longing for the presence of God and search their depths. Try to discern and understand what they say about the anointing of God. We are seeking the Lord in these pages.

BOLDNESS TO COME INTO GOD'S PRESENCE

There are so many who have tried to come up with ways to describe the anointing of the Lord. Many are confusing and conflicting, but some are helpful. For instance, some have studied the word *anointing* and tried to help us understand its increasing flow by comparing it to the parts of the tabernacle of Moses. They compare the tabernacle's Outer Court to David's words in Psalm 63, when he states that his soul thirsts for God—David's desire for the Lord gets him to the periphery. But then his flesh is also longing for God, indicating that David has moved from being distant and looking toward God to stepping into the Inner Court, or the Holy Place. And when his spirit is seeking God, they

"Lord, it is Your tangible presence that I seek, when Your invisible presence is almost on the brink of being visible, when Your presence so saturates the atmosphere around me that it's as if I can touch and feel Your presence!"

make the analogy that he has moved into the place of the Holy of Holies, where the immediate presence of the Lord was.

The key is the longing and the seeking for God, but how do we do that? How do we begin? How do we obtain this wonderful gift that God has for us? The safe and sure way to begin is to go to God in prayer, to submit and humble ourselves in prayer before Him. Yet so often, when we first begin to pray, it feels as though God is so far away. Does He hear? Does He care? Will He respond? Will He reach out to me? Are my words having any impact? Where is He?

However, regardless of how that prayer feels to us, as we begin to pray, let me encourage you that it begins to crucify our flesh. In other words, as we seek God, it takes the power out of my wants and gets me out of self-consciousness and into a place of God-consciousness. When I am self-conscious, the first result is fear. But when I become God-conscious, the first fruit is boldness. Fear holds me back from coming to Him, but as I seek and stay in His presence, I discover that my prayers don't have to be so perfect. They don't have to be so magnificent. God is not looking for lustrous prayers with just the right words. That gives me boldness that I can approach His presence freely. I can come as I am without fear and just be honest.

We discover that what God is looking for is surrender. Will I give up? Will I give over everything to Him? Will I surrender myself? So as we stay there, seeking the presence of God, and we move from self-consciousness to God-consciousness, the presence of the Lord begins to confront our disobedience and speaks to us that what we need is more of the Lord in our lives. And as we cry out to the Lord, who had first seemed so far away, we sense His presence coming near, and at some point there is what I call a breakthrough. Suddenly, we feel that our prayers and the thoughts of our heart are going beyond the room, and God is hearing because He is near.

And when we sense that breakthrough into His presence, it is as though the river begins to flow, and there's a flood. There are more words that come. We don't have to labor and struggle to talk to the Lord, but we sense a true relationship with God. We sense our inheritance from Him. We know that God is eager to have His children talk to Him. So then the idols in my heart begin to die. We begin to let go and say, "God, what I thought was so important to talk to You about I now see is a lesser priority. Right now, I just want to hear from You."

By way of our analogy, we have moved and been ushered from the Outer Place into the Inner Place, which is why the apostle Paul said, "I die daily" (1 Corinthians 15:31). He is saying, "I must constantly surrender myself to You, O God." We think so often of repentance as just being the initial step for surrender to the Lordship of Christ, leading to salvation. But do you know that the spirit of repentance has to be a part of our lives all along, so we remain teachable and pliable in the presence of the Lord? A spirit of repentance keeps us in that place where we can hear His voice and His instruction. Repentance is a recognition of how great our need is for God, and it becomes a lifestyle, a living motive to be genuine and real and bare before God, in order that we might hear more of the voice of the Lord speaking us. It is the loving God coming to us and giving loving instruction as to what not to do and what to do, when to be quiet and when to apologize, and when we need to change our attitudes.

Here's my point: When we talk about the manifest presence of God, He does not anoint a vessel that's full of dirt, that's full of self, that's clinging to our own ways, that's justifying selfish pleasure and sin. The anointing of God leads to the formation of Jesus in our lives, and He is "altogether lovely." Our Messiah is not going to inhabit where the dirt and cobwebs are, or where we have fabricated our own conditions and rules for when we will obey His voice. We are to be "a vessel for honor, sanctified and useful for the Master, prepared for every good work" (2 Timothy 2:21).

OUR SOUL PANTS FOR HIS PRESENCE

Let us remind ourselves that as believers we have been given the right to use the precious, powerful Name of Jesus. We are not left out in the Outer Court or even in the Inner Court, but we are privileged and called into the presence of the living God. Our God has given us the power to rout and uproot the kingdom of darkness with just a word. Do you realize that we have that kind of authority in the anointing? We don't have to plead with

When we talk about the manifest presence of God, He does not anoint a vessel that's full of dirt, that's full of self, that's clinging to our own ways, that's justifying selfish pleasure and sin.

or beg the enemy, but when we speak the Name of Jesus and believe that God is working, the enemy must leave. Every hindrance and distraction must depart from His presence.

We are asking God to take us through this journey. So Paul says, "I die daily." Our attitude must be that of the lover in the Song of Solomon, *Have you seen my beloved? Can you tell me where my beloved is?* That's what we're doing. We're searching high and low for our Beloved. Our spirit man is running through the Word of God. And we're saying, "Have you seen Jesus? If you see Him, tell Him that I'm looking for Him." Be encouraged that when you read the Song of Solomon, the lover says about the beloved, "And I found him." As we seek and thirst for His presence, we will find Him as we dwell in His Word and His promises.

I love how David draws us into longing and thirsting for the presence of God. We find that so beautifully described in Psalm 42:1–2: "As the deer pants for the water brooks, so pants my soul for You, O God. My soul thirsts for God, for the living God." To be panting is to be "out of breath, thirsting, longing, and seeking" for the refreshing streams of the presence of God. Acts 3:19 tells us that times of refreshing come from the presence of the Lord. We sense that in the presence of God there is something that waters and refreshes. It's a quenching of my soul. The presence of God comes to put out the flames of anxiety and the fire of worry.

So our inner being is desiring the presence of God as a deer pants for water. First, the deer cannot possibly live without water and its refreshment. But sometimes the deer is also panting for that stream of water because a predator is chasing it. In our lives, we look for the refreshing of the Lord not just to quench the dryness of our soul and flesh and spirit, but an adversary pursues us. There is a lion, as a roaring lion, an adversary who goes to and fro, seeking to devour, to steal and kill and to destroy (1 Peter 5:8). And because we're not just pursuing after God, but we're also fleeing the work of the tempter, we must go to the water brooks.

And the thing that blesses my soul is that when we get into the water, the hounds of hell, so to speak, cannot follow our scent. That natural scent gets lost and washed in the water, and we begin to pick up the divine fragrance of God's presence. We begin to take on the fragrance and the aroma of the living resurrected Jesus. We have to get to the refreshing in our spirits. We have to get to the waters. We have to be in the presence of God, because the enemy is thrown off there and cannot follow us in that place.

This is why David writes in Psalm 32:7, "You are my hiding place; You shall preserve me in trouble; You shall surround me with songs of deliverance." In the presence of God, He keeps us. We are in a safe pavilion. We are preserved from trouble and encompassed with songs of deliverance!

Then David gives us more to long for our God as the voice of the Lord says, "I will instruct you and teach you in the way you should go; I will guide you with My eye." What an amazing promise! We are allowed to begin to see with the all-seeing, omniscient eye of God. We begin to see things in the spirit. We will have an inner awareness and an inner knowing that God is revealing to us.

By way of example of this, I was recently reading one of my old books and came upon a page where I had written a note dated 2001 that I had no recollection of writing. Apparently I had watched a television program with Bishop Jakes, whom I only knew as a television personality at the time. He had made a statement about a ministry that he was about to launch, which drew my interest, and I jotted a note down on that page of the book. Over thirteen years later, I opened to this page and found the forgotten note that described very closely the ministry I am doing now at the Potter's House. You see, the Lord sometimes will give us glimpses of what He has for us. In this case, it was an assignment that He was entrusting to me and that He revealed to me long ahead of time. For you, it may be a country to which

We don't forget that taste of the glory
of God, and we're never the same, because
we recognize that closeness and that
dearness of His presence. When we're
there, our heart can respond to His voice,
"Be still, and know that I am God"
(Psalm 46:10). We know Him.

you're drawn to work or a mission opportunity. It may be a service you're going to give long before you meet that opportunity. God says, "I will guide you with My eye." And the beauty is that His eye doesn't have a speck in it. He's not nearsighted or farsighted, but He's the perfect all-seeing, all-knowing God. What a promise for us to have from the Lord!

WHEN GOD'S LOVE FLOODS OVER US

David has taken us into our hiding place in the presence of God. We are seeking His power and glory and willing to die to self and our flesh so that His anointing, His presence, might be there to speak to us and to lead us on. When we get to that inner place in God that we compare to the Holy of Holies, we stop telling God our issues and complaints, because we're in that place where He begins to talk to us. I can't tell you how to get there in a formulaic way, though. It's not by doing A, B, C, and then God moves. There are suggested patterns, but I'm very nervous about people who reduce the anointing to a formula, stating that "if you just do this, you're going to receive this." God cannot be limited to formulas. This is all about our ongoing relationship with Him.

What I have discovered is that sometimes the way we see God move is when we're out of songs, we're out of prayers, and we don't know what to do. I compare it to what David said in Psalm 42, that when I get to this point, "Deeps calls unto deep at the noise of Your waterfalls; all Your waves and billows have gone over me" (v. 7). It's something in the very depths of God. Out of the holy core nature of God, there is a calling to what God has deposited in me. David says, in other words, "God, You're just flooding me over with love." He adds, "The LORD will command His lovingkindness in the daytime, and in the night His song shall be with me." That's what happens sometimes when we get there. It's no longer about what the earlier experiences were, but it's that my spirit is able to commune with God.

And so now we're not just longing and thirsting as David expressed in Psalm 63; now we're drinking. We're just drinking that water and taking it in. It's where words are inadequate. It's where we feel so full. If we ever experience this in the Lord, we don't forget it. We don't forget that taste of the glory of God, and we're never the same, because we recognize that closeness and that dearness of His presence. When we're there, our heart can respond to His voice, "Be still, and know that I am God" (Psalm 46:10). We know Him.

"Awake! Put on Your Strength! Loose Yourself!"

Then the word comes to us in Isaiah 52:1–2: "Awake, awake! Put on your strength, O Zion; put on your beautiful garments, O Jerusalem, the holy city! For the uncircumcised and the unclean shall no longer come to you. Shake yourself from the dust, arise; sit down, O Jerusalem! Loose yourself from the bonds of your neck, O captive daughter of Zion!" God is inviting us to come into His presence, and the more time we spend with God, the more we lose our old scent that those evil hounds can identify, and the more we get the fragrance of God that is to characterize our life.

This word *awake* calls us to prayer. It is a summons to come into the presence of the Lord. We find strength to put on in the presence of the Lord. We find garments of the priesthood to put on that have the anointing oil with its perfume. It's not ours personally, and it's not about how great we are—it about the anointing oil that is on the garment we put on. Yes, we are privileged and blessed to serve the Lord, but there is an anointing for every believer, and all of us have a service to give, and it all belongs to Him. One service is not more important than another.

Every believer is to seek to know and receive the anointing that God has for them. We need the presence of God to embody all that we do and all that we are. The Word declares, "Put on your strength: put on your beautiful garments." You have a covering. You have a provision. You have a power. There is an ability to preserve you. You're not limited. Do not be as Adam was when he sinned and was afraid and hid himself from the presence of God. We have a place in God. We're not limited to our self-covering.

He said, "O Jerusalem . . . the uncircumcised and the unclean shall no longer come to you." That means that those who don't want to obey the law of God, who are rebellious and stubborn and don't want to be in the move and flow of God, will not be able to enter into this place. They won't be interested in the anointing and will no longer come to us. So what you need to do is shake yourself from the dust—from the things that cling, the low things,

the meager things, the accusations, the condemna-
tions, the finger-pointing, the yoke of lies. Shake off
the "I can't," the "I never will," the "it's impossible for
me," the blame toward parents who didn't do something or that we don't have this or that. Dust is just
something that lies on the surface and clings, but
dust is not rooted in anything. God says to shake it
off and get up. "Shake yourself!" Whatever it is that
is clinging to us and holding us back from the presence of the Lord, we must shake off and arise and
move to another plane.

"Loose yourself from the bonds of your neck!"
God's Word and His presence is a right now word,
and He has put the *rhema* power in our mouths that
we can be free from the things that would bind us
and keep us in bondage. "Loose yourself!" I thank
God for what He does supernaturally, but He has
made it possible, and we can be free. We can be free!
The liberator is in you! "Loose yourself from the
bonds of your neck, O captive daughter of Zion."

When it comes to temptations to sinful pleasures and bondages to sin, we are told that when we
find that place of God's presence and press our way
to stay there, crying out to God and talking to the
Lord and moving closer and near to Him, what happens is we get strength to resist those things. We get
strength to resist wrong desires. I'm not saying that
we never fail. But when we put on the garments of
righteousness, disobedience is not able to claim us
and live in our lives. And those who don't want to
know this way that God has provided for us won't
come with us, so we won't have fellowship with the
kingdom of darkness and wickedness. We don't
always have to push them away. They'll either come

*Shake off
the "I can't,"
the "I never
will," the "it's
impossible for
me," the blame
toward parents
who didn't do
something or
that we don't
have this
or that.*

because they love the light of Christ in our life, or they'll walk away. Then we find rest and peace in Jesus.

And that brings us to the place of fellowship that the prophet Isaiah describes: "How beautiful upon the mountains are the feet of him who brings good news, who proclaims peace, who brings glad tidings of good things, who proclaims salvation, who says to Zion, 'Your God reigns!'" (Isaiah 52:7). That's the bottom line. That's the place where we "sit down" in His presence. We've loosed ourselves from the hindrances, and now we get to enjoy His presence. We let "our God reigns" stretch us and pull our head up and straighten our back and support us. My God reigns! Our God reigns!

THE ANOINTING AND THE FRUIT OF THE SPIRIT

So there is an awakening for us in the Word of God, and we're willing to do what it takes to press our way into His presence. First Corinthians 9:27 says, "But I discipline my body and bring it into subjection, lest, when I have preached to others, I myself should become disqualified." God doesn't make us do this, but the choice is ours, and we want to take our flesh and submit it to Him, because when we call on Him, He answers us. He really does, and He says, "I will show you great and mighty things!" He'll give us new vision, and we'll see His glory and His power!

It's not yesterday's anointing that we want. We want the anointing for today and the glory of God that is available for us now. What is that glory? It's the presence of God. I want to see His glory. Remember when Moses said to the Lord, "Please, show me Your glory" (Exodus 33:18)? Read that entire chapter, and you'll see it is all about the presence of the Lord going with the people. And God replied to Moses, "I will make all My goodness pass before you." What is that? The Lord is saying, "I will let My nature come before you." What is the nature of the Lord? It is the attributes of God, the characteristics of God.

We find those attributes of God working out practically in our lives through the fruit of the Spirit (Galatians 5:22–23). What are those but the characteristics or nature of God working into our lives and producing fruit through the presence of the Holy Spirit. If God is going to dwell in us and He is anointing us with His power, our lives must be a place where He loves to come and dwell. As we pray and make ourselves available to the Lord, He comes into our heart and begins to work on us, making us pliable and malleable to His will, a fit vessel for His anointing. After all, what would it be like to have the power of the Spirit that comes and is manifested through the spiritual gifts when our character and nature is not like God? So when we invite the Lord to come, His nature begins to come in and transform our life through His Spirit. When Christ comes in, the fullness of Christ's nature comes, and as our nature becomes like His, the anointing can come. God will not anoint what is not according to His own nature.

So let us evaluate ourselves. Rather than boast, "I am anointed because I had such and such an experience," we should rather ask, "In my daily life, do I see the love, joy, peace, longsuffering, kindness, goodness, faithfulness, gentleness, and self-control that demonstrate the presence of the Holy Spirit?" Let's make sure we are bringing the fruit of the Spirit and the true anointing together.

What We Are Anointed For

Now, what are we anointed for? Acts 1:8 states, "But you shall receive power when the Holy Spirit has come upon you; and you shall be witnesses to Me in Jerusalem, and in all Judea and Samaria, and to the end of the earth." Jesus was saying, "I give you My presence in your life for you to witness what God did through My life and what I went through." It is not to empower us to tell others all the things we've gone through and how we've arrived at where we are in the kingdom of God today. Yes, what we have personally experienced is a testimony to the power of God, but the Holy Spirit was not given so that we can tell *our* story. Jesus didn't die to make my personal story captivating. He didn't die so that I would have something worth publishing about my life. He did not shed His blood so my experiences would "wow" people. It's not about the difficulties we've endured, or the victories we've had, or the service we've given.

The anointing we receive is about the good news, the freedom that we have in Christ. That's the only thing worth telling. Everything else is a footnote. Everything else is an epilogue. Do you know what God went through for you? Do you know the price He paid for you? Do you know Jesus' sacrifice?

Otherwise, we are in danger of boasting in ourselves and singing about how we got over into the kingdom. I love that song, but that's not the gospel.

The second thing that we are anointed for is seen in Leviticus 14, where it teaches about the cleansing ritual for a healed leper. The priest would go outside the camp to the leper, sprinkle the leper with blood seven times, then he would bring the leper into the camp, and in that inner time the leper would be sprinkled again with the blood seven times. I apply that sequence to my life in this way: I am the leper, the diseased one who is outside of the camp of Israel and cannot come into the fellowship. I am at a distance, stained with my own selfishness and sin, but my great High Priest, Jesus Christ, came all the way from heaven and brought me into the camp. He sprinkled me with His blood outside the camp, then brought me into the camp through His blood, and then He took the oil and applied the oil to the tip of my ear, the thumb of my right hand, and the big toe of my right foot (vv. 16–17). The ear was anointed so I could hear the voice of the Lord. The oil was placed on my thumb so I could work right, and on my big toe so I could walk right before the Lord.

So sprinkle the blood, sprinkle the blood, then apply the oil. Very simple. Let's be certain that we don't try to apply the oil before we apply the blood. The blood was applied outside the camp, then we were brought into the camp and the blood was applied again, which is followed by the oil. If we try to apply the oil, and we've not applied the blood, we don't have a chance to hear right, to work right, or to walk right. Our lives get out of order.

What would it be like to have the power of the Spirit that comes and is manifested through the spiritual gifts when our character and nature is not like God?

My concern is that we see people who claim or perhaps appear to be exercising a spiritual gift with power, but there's something fundamental missing in their lives, something missing in their character and purity. So as we seek the anointing and desire to walk in the power of the Spirit, let's make sure that we have the sequence right. The blood of animals that they used was a type and a shadow of the blood of Jesus, the perfect Lamb of God. So that when John the Baptist saw Jesus coming, he said, "Behold—not an ox, not a bull—but behold the Lamb of God." Who does what? "Who takes away the sins of the world" (John 1:29). That's where the invitation that we have begins.

No Shortage of the Anointing upon Us

I am going to close this chapter with one more encouraging scripture to long for the anointing. Ecclesiastics 9:8 says, "Let your garments always be white, and let your head lack no oil." That means we are to present a pure life, a pure testimony before the Lord, and we are to not let our head lack the oil of gladness. Let's have no shortage of the anointing on our heads. That is my prayer and the longing of my heart, and I trust it is your prayer as well.

"Lord, let there be no lack of oil on my head. No lack of understanding. No lack of wisdom. Don't let me lack insight. Don't let me lack, so that I can make the right judgments. Don't let me lack in purity. Don't let me lack, O God, in peace and joy and love and longsuffering and gentleness and goodness and meekness and self-control. Let there be no lack. Let my head, my mind, my thoughts, and my spirit be dripping in the anointing. In Jesus' Name. Amen."

If we try to apply the oil, and we've not applied the blood, we don't have a chance to hear right, to work right, or to walk right. Our lives get out of order.

YOU CANNOT PARENT THAT CHILD,

love that husband, care for that elderly parent,

submit to that boss, teach that Sunday school class,

or lead that small-group Bible study.

GOD SPECIALIZES IN THE IMPOSSIBLE,

God specialize

so that when the victory is won and the task is complete, we cannot take any credit. Others know we didn't do it, and we know we didn't do it. We must always remember that we can only live the Christian life and serve God through the power of His Holy Spirit. As soon as we think we can handle it on our own, we become useless to Him. We have to be willing to get out of the way, let God take over, and let Him overshadow us.

NANCY LEIGH DEMOSS

n the impossible...

CHAPTER SIX

THE MAIN INGREDIENT OF THE ANOINTING OIL

Moreover the LORD spoke to Moses, saying:

"Also take for yourself quality spices—five hundred shekels

of liquid myrrh, half as much sweet-smelling cinnamon

(two hundred and fifty shekels),

two hundred and fifty shekels of sweet-smelling cane [calamus],

five hundred shekels of cassia,

according to the shekel of the sanctuary, and a hin of olive oil.

And you shall make from these a holy anointing oil."

EXODUS 30:22–25

hen it comes to the anointing of the Holy Spirit, in some circles it is typically dismissed as having been relevant only to the days of the apostles in the New Testament church, while in other circles it is popular to focus on the power and the manifestations of the gifts of the Spirit. While I fully believe that the anointing is as relevant today as it was for Peter and Paul, and though I fully believe in the power and gifts of the Spirit for today, my focus is on the anointing as being the presence of God in our lives.

Why is that important? Because we want the power and the gifts to be aligned with the nature of Jesus in us. If the anointing is operating in our lives, we must be in Christ, because the anointing, the presence of God, will not anoint my flesh. The anointing may leave because of sin in my life, but the gift may remain. The gift may still be there, but the anointing may not be on it. And that is where churches and our lives so often get out of order, because the gifts then begin to flow out of our carnal natures for selfish purposes that end up damaging others and the body of Christ.

At the end of the last chapter, we considered the fruit of the Spirit (Galatians 5:22–23), because the anointing anoints the nature of Christ. In other words, the presence of the Spirit of Christ accompanies the nature of Christ. So I need to get His nature in me. His life must be formed in my character. If I'm cranky and can't get along with anyone, or if I'm full of myself and so proud of my talents, that's not the nature of Christ, no matter how much I might talk about power and manifesting my gift. I need the nature of God, because the anointing will honor that nature. They go together, so it's not just the gifts, not just the wonders, not just the amazement, not just the excitement, not just the miracles—I'm thankful for them, but I need the nature of Jesus. I need love, joy, peace, longsuffering, kindness, goodness, faithfulness, gentleness, and self-control to be the hallmark of my life.

Are we walking in the nature of the Spirit of Christ and displaying His presence when people come into our presence? Are they getting the fragrance of God, or is it us? Remember in Acts 4:13, the Jewish officials "saw the boldness of Peter and John . . . And they realized they have been with Jesus." The apostles had been in such fellowship with the presence of Jesus that they picked up the very fragrance of God. If we want to talk about the anointing, let it begin with whether our nature bears the fruit of His presence.

The Lord knows that when we have a broken heart, whether it's from shame, hurt, or disappointment, that can be a barrier or a hindrance to the anointing.

THE ANOINTING IN THE MIDST OF BROKENNESS

Today's church culture struggles with reconciling the fact that Jesus said, "If anyone desires to come after Me, let him deny himself, and take up his cross daily, and follow Me" (Luke 9:23), and that He has promised us an abundant life (John 10:10). But the two go together. I find the blending of the two in the aspect of brokenness that is symbolized in the first ingredient of the anointing oil, the myrrh, which we started to look at in Chapter 3. It's something that we see all throughout Scripture—that in sorrow there is joy. It's not somehow a detour around sorrow. It's not a detour around brokenness. It was by going through the brokenness, going through the pain of it, and going through the heartache and the disdain that Jesus endured the cross. He despised the shame and endured the cross "for the joy that was set before Him" (Hebrews 12:2). He knew where He was going, and to get there He had to go through the cross, which led to the joy of providing for our salvation.

The enemy may try to tell you it's not worth taking up your cross every day and following Jesus. He'll tell you it won't work out, and that it certainly has nothing to do with the abundant life Jesus promised. But if you know where you're going, as Jesus did, you'll go right dead center through it because of what's been set on the other side. It's joy in the midst of sorrow. It's not joy next door to and down the street from, but joy in the midst of sorrow. Don't let the enemy tell you that you've missed God because there's some pain and disappointments in your life. God has said that He will take us through. The two go together, the joy and the sorrow. It's not one despite the other.

God knows when we have a broken heart, and that to be brokenhearted can come from at least two different sources. It can be from the hurts and disappointments and bitter experiences that sometimes occur among believers. There can be misunderstandings and unkindness and even abuses that lead to such deep hurt and disappointment that we're hesitant to approach the Lord, which is a hindrance to the anointing. We are hesitant to reach out to try again, to trust again, because of violations to our spirit, which leads to woundedness.

What I love is that God has extraordinary means of dealing with the brokenhearted. "The righteous cry out, and the LORD hears, and delivers them out of all their troubles" (Psalm 34:17). In the Hebrew, to *deliver* means to "snatch out." God rescues, snatches out, and delivers them from all their troubles. It goes on, "The LORD is near to those who have a broken heart, and saves such as have a contrite spirit." In other words, He knows my heart is limping. Imagine, if you can, a cracked heart limping on crutches. The Lord knows that when we have a broken heart, whether it's from shame, hurt, or disappointment, that can be a barrier or a hindrance to the anointing. It can make it hard for us to want to be in His presence. So the Lord says, "I know you're having a struggle to get over what happened and the wounds and pain, and I know the enemy's trying to use that to keep you out of the body of Christ and from coming into My presence. So, I'll just come near you to save you."

As painful as it can be to be brokenhearted, there is nothing to compare to when the Lord comes near with His presence to soothe our brow, catch our tears, dry our eyes, lift us up, and carry us. In Psalm 34, David was about to complain about the wicked being successful, but when God came near he saw through the enemy's lies and began to glorify God. In affliction, he found glory. God comes near and heals the broken heart and saves the contrite spirit. He knows our disappointments, failures, pain, and brokenness, because He knows and loves us.

Jesus said, quoting the prophet Isaiah, "The Spirit of the Lord GOD is upon Me, because the LORD has anointed Me to preach good tidings to the poor; He has sent Me to heal the brokenhearted" (Isaiah 61:1). How wonderful! He had been sent to "heal" the broken heart—not to patch it up, but to make it whole again. That's what the Lord does. Those things may be a hindrance to the anointing and the presence of God, but the Lord brings healing through His presence.

Then consider the words of Isaiah 57:15: "For thus says the High and Lofty One Who inhabits eternity, whose name is Holy: 'I dwell in the high and holy place, with him who has a contrite [broken] and humble spirit.'" Now this is not the "brokenness" that results from what other people have done to us, but it is a voluntary, intentional contriteness and humbleness in the person who dwells in the presence of the High and Lofty One. God is with us "to revive the spirit of the humble, and to revive the heart of the contrite ones." Whatever has brought us to this point in life, He is here to bring us life, to resuscitate, and to put us back together again. And so we experience God in the midst of suffering, in the midst of what would be brokenness, and we understand that He is near us. He defends us, rescues us, delivers us, snatches us out, and He does all this in order to save us. He heals our broken heart.

Myrrh—the First and Main Ingredient in the Anointing Oil

Brokenness is bitterness, which brings me back to the anointing oil as described in Exodus 30:22–25. "Moreover the LORD spoke to Moses, saying: 'Also take for yourself quality spices—five hundred shekels of liquid myrrh, half as much sweet-smelling cinnamon (two hundred and fifty shekels), two hundred and fifty shekels of sweet-smelling cane [calamus], five hundred shekels of cassia, according to the shekel of the sanctuary, and a hin of olive oil. And you shall make from these a holy anointing oil.'" God's instructions were very specific—they were not to make any variations or substitutes for these five ingredients. He even said to use the scale in the sanctuary, to not go by any other measurement.

Interestingly, *myrrh* comes from a word that means "distilled," and the root of that word means "bitter" or "mara." Remember that after Naomi had suffered the death of her husband and two sons, she told people, "Do not call me Naomi, call me Mara [bitter], for the Almighty has dealt very bitterly with me" (Ruth 1:20). Myrrh is the gum or resin that comes from a shrub or plant and is very bitter to the taste. It doesn't flow out—every now and then it oozes out. It's similar to our lives when we're just going along and suddenly everything seems to fall in on us. It doesn't taste good. It's not good. Trouble is not good. Standing at a graveside and burying your children are not good, and losing a loved one is not good. Losing a job doesn't taste good. It has a bitter taste, and we don't have to be unrealistic and untruthful about it or try to spiritualize it by saying "It is well."

Myrrh is bitter in the mouth, but it had a highly valued fragrance. And that is what trouble does. It's difficult going down. The taste is horrific, but at the same time, the benefit of it and the result of it is so worth it on the other end. Which is why God says we need that as a main ingredient in our lives. What kind of believer would we be if we never had the myrrh, the suffering? The apostle Paul wrote, "All who desire to live godly in Christ Jesus will suffer persecution" (2 Timothy 3:12). It is a principal ingredient in our making to be disciples and servants and followers of Christ. It does not feel good. We don't have to put a false name on it, but we can see it for what it really is. Yes, it's suffering, and it's bitter, but it's suffering with a purpose of glory. It's suffering with a meaning. We are not gluttons for punishment. We

WHATEVER HAS BROUGHT US

TO THIS POINT IN LIFE,

THE LORD IS HERE TO BRING US LIFE,

TO RESUSCITATE, AND TO PUT US

BACK TOGETHER AGAIN.

are not looking for martyrdom. We are not somehow addicted to misery, but we understand that when it happens, in the midst of it, God will show Himself strong.

When we look at the anointing oil, myrrh is the principal ingredient. It's the largest measure of the components that go into making the anointed oil for the priest. The priest is the one who is going to be the intercessor between God and the people. The priest is the one who is going to carry the people's concerns to God, so the priest needs to have myrrh, the symbolic bitterness, in the anointing. Because when we haven't gone through anything difficult, it's easy to be judgmental. But after we've had our major issues that we perhaps don't want to tell anyone about, we see others in a different light and treat them with compassion. We're not so quick to judge their health, their marriage, their children, or their finances. We're quicker to come alongside and genuinely join with them.

The priest who's going to carry the people's burden cannot be in a place of arrogance and loftiness. They have to know what it is to suffer and cry sometimes. We need to know that in the anointing, which is for every believer as part of the priesthood of believers, there's some suffering. We have to have that myrrh in our life. But the myrrh is not on our flesh. The anointing oil is on the priest's garment, and the garment is the ministry the Lord has given us. I'm called as a believer to wear this priestly garment of service to God, to live this life, to walk this walk, and with the wearing of the garment comes the suffering. It comes with the anointing.

The anointing is on the garment or the mantle, so I can't get lifted up and say, "I have the anointing and the power. I have the inside track on God." No, I don't. We see it in the mantle that was passed down from Elijah to Elisha, the garment that Hannah sewed and sent to the temple every year to fit on Samuel, and the garment that Jesus wore so the woman with the issue of blood could touch the hem and be healed. The anointing is on the garment or the mantle. It's not about me. When we remember that, we realize we are just privileged and honored to wear the anointing for a season.

It's the anointing of the Lord. It's His presence. It's a garment that will never fit me. The garment will always be too big for me. I just get in it the best I can, but I never fill it out. I never come to the full stature. I'm always trying to grow up to the full measure of Christ. I'm always trying to get more of Him. I'm always trying to be able to fit the pattern and fit the measurements and receive the grace that goes along with it.

"No Cross, No Crown"

So the anointing is on the mantle, and suffering and brokenness are a part of it. And often that brokenness is something we voluntarily endure so that there can be a fresh oil. As we're seeking the presence of the Lord for His outpouring, we find that the cross of Calvary cuts us. When we receive a revelation of God's love, it pierces and breaks us open, and when it breaks that outer shell, the flesh nature, the anointing can be poured out and available to assist others.

Then in the brokenness we are sometimes called to pray. There is a crushing in it. Bishop Jakes talks about that crushing and that breaking in his book *Anointing Fall on Me*. He compares us to the persecuted church in Smyrna in Revelation 2:8–11. Please read it in your Bible. Interestingly, *Smyrna* means "myrrh." The persecuted church is broken, but we're going through. The Lord knows our works because His presence is near, and He sees us. He knows our tribulations and poverty, which means poorness in spirit, brokenness in spirit, but we are rich because in the midst of the brokenness there is joy. Jesus knows about the harsh things spoken against us. He tells us to not fear the things we will suffer or the trials and tribulations. If we are faithful unto death, we will be given a crown of life.

While he was imprisoned in the Tower of London for his faith in 1670, William Penn penned the phrase, "No cross, no crown." The two go together. So in the anointing we voluntarily move ourselves to a place where we begin to intercede for others, and as Jesus did, we learn obedience through the suffering that involves (Hebrews 5:8). The anointing is not just for what's going on in our life, but we can enter a place of myrrh, a place of bitterness and suffering for others. One author writes about it as the prayer of suffering. It's the kind of prayer that Jesus prayed on Calvary when He said, "Father, forgive them, for they do not know what they do" (Luke 23:24). It's the kind of prayer that Stephen prayed for those who stoned him. It's a real place of brokenness in the spirit where we can enter in and begin to petition God for others.

And that's when the anointing and the presence of God has a purpose. We get to a place where it's not just the words we say in counsel to others, but it's the tears that we shed with them. It has a redemptive purpose in it. In other words, it accomplishes something because we bring the brokenness that lifts them into the arms of Christ. That's the care we want. It's not about the certificates and degrees on the wall, or the number of times we witness to someone, or how wonderfully we exercise a spiritual gift. But we're in a place where we can share and graciously serve the Word of God, so that it has redemption to it and people begin to say, "Tell me more about the Father and His love. Tell me about what Jesus suffered for me. Tell me how you are going through that situation with so much grace."

That's what we're called to do. We are the people who should attract others to Jesus. We are to be anointed people of grace. And what is grace? It's the undeserved favor and help of God. That's the presence of God. That's the anointing where the glory of God invades, pervades, and takes over—the manifest presence of God right in our situation.

"The Glory Which Shall Be Revealed in Us"

The apostle Paul takes this principle of taking up our cross to a level that is impossible for us to comprehend in the natural. He says, "I now rejoice in my sufferings for you, and fill up in my flesh what is lacking in the afflictions of Christ, for the sake of His body, which is the church" (Colossians 1:24). Paul is not suggesting that Christ's suffering was somehow deficient. He's not saying that the blood of Jesus was inadequate in providing a

The anointing is on the garment or the mantle, so I can't get lifted up and say, "I have the anointing and the power. I have the inside track on God."

substitutionary atonement for the salvation of the world. He is saying that even though Christ suffered, we are invited to drink deeply of the Master's cup and share in His suffering. He is saying that as believers we endure the suffering that Christ would be enduring if He were still in the world. Instead of facing these difficulties with dread, Paul saw his troubles as a reason for joy, because they were producing an eternal reward (2 Corinthians 4:17). He shows us that Jesus demonstrated a clear example of a compatibility of grace and suffering and how they go together.

Paul also said, "For I consider that the sufferings of this present time are not worthy to be compared with the glory which shall be revealed in us" (Romans 8:18). He is saying, "I stopped and considered all I've gone through, being beaten, in peril, shipwrecked, left for dead, imprisoned, being mistreated and abandoned by my own countrymen. Yes, there have been disappointments and detours, persecutions, tribulations, and afflictions. It didn't always feel good; sometimes it was extremely painful. But the sufferings of this present time are not worthy and don't carry the weight to even be in the same ballpark with the glory that will be revealed in us. There is no basis of comparison. There's nothing that I can analyze or synthesize, break apart, or put together that has the same constitution. It's not just glory out there. It's not just a 'pillar of cloud' like what went before the people of Israel in the wilderness, but this is all the glory. This is going to be the presence and the power and the glory of God."

If you think Moses was radiating glory when he came down from speaking with the Lord on Mount Zion (Exodus 34:30), when the glory of God is revealed in your life, the whole world has to take notice. And I'm not just talking about on that great getting up morning when we meet the Lord in the air. I'm talking about when the captivity in your life is changed, as when Job began to pray and the captivity of his friends turned around in an instant (Job 42). When God turns it around, the glory is just showing. You're wearing the glory. The glory is radiating. That's the victory of God. You can wear the glory, because it's going to be revealed *in you. In me.* Not just on my neighbor, but *in me.* Yes, the glory of God. And Paul says that this glory will be "revealed." It becomes a testimony and a witness to the power of

Jesus Christ. We don't see the glory, but it's going to be revealed. Just keep watching; it's going to be revealed at the right time.

I hope you see that the Lord is near to the brokenhearted. The Lord is close to those who are humble and of a contrite spirit. The presence of God is with us; His anointing is for us. The presence of God is here healing our hearts and lifting our heads, bringing glory. Since we are in His presence, we ought to embrace and love Him. We are seeking after our God. We cry out, "My soul is thirsting, my flesh is longing, and my spirit is seeking Him. When shall I come before the living God? When will He show Himself strong on my behalf? He will not despise a broken and contrite spirit."

Whatever the disappointments and hurts and sufferings are in your life, I challenge you to give them to the Lord right now. Right where you're reading, make that your altar. Cast your cares upon Him, for He cares for you. Seek the washing of the blood. Seek the washing of the Word. Before the anointing of the oil, have your heart sprinkled with the blood of Jesus, the Lamb of God. Ask Him to heal your broken heart, and be loosed from all that has held you back. The Lord hears your cry and will deliver you out of all your trouble. He's bringing you out. He's snatching you out. He's bringing you through. Receive His joy in the midst of sorrow. Thank God that you can glory in tribulation. Thank Him for the sweet fragrance of His presence even though the taste is bitter. Humble yourself before Him. Be still and know that He is God. Declare that you can't live without Him. Just softly pray, "Lord, I need Your presence. Amen."

The sufferings of this present time are not worthy and don't carry the weight to even be in the same ballpark with the glory that will be revealed in us.

WILL GOD EVER ASK YOU TO DO SOMETHING

you are not able to do?

THE ANSWER IS YES—ALL THE TIME!

God

It must be that way, for God's glory and kingdom. If we function according to our ability alone, we get the glory; if we function according to the power of the Spirit within us, God gets the glory. He wants to reveal Himself to a watching world.

HENRY T. BLACKABY

gets the glory

CHAPTER SEVEN

THE ECONOMICAL MOVE OF GOD

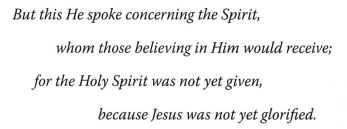

But this He spoke concerning the Spirit,

whom those believing in Him would receive;

for the Holy Spirit was not yet given,

because Jesus was not yet glorified.

JOHN 7:39

hen it comes to understanding the anointing, it is easy to overlook the actual ingredients in the anointing oil, but in doing so we miss valuable instruction on why the Lord specifically chose to include what He did. He never does anything without a reason, so the more that we come to understand His ways, the deeper we come to understand His purposes. This is the anointing oil as described in Exodus 30:22–25: "Moreover the LORD spoke to Moses, saying: 'Also take for yourself quality spices—five hundred shekels of liquid myrrh, half as much sweet-smelling cinnamon (two hundred and fifty shekels), two hundred and fifty shekels of sweet-smelling cane [calamus], five hundred shekels of cassia, according to the shekel of the sanctuary, and a hin of olive oil. And you shall make from these a holy anointing oil.'"

I begin with a brief overview of the ingredients, which will be followed with more details regarding each. Five hundred shekels of liquid myrrh was the primary ingredient. As we saw in the previous chapter, myrrh symbolizes pain, misery, and suffering. In essence, it symbolizes the death of Christ. Then comes the second ingredient, two hundred and fifty shekels of sweet-smelling cinnamon, which is half the amount of myrrh. That indicates to me that there's twice the bitter to the sweet. Twice as much of the tough times, the rainy days when we endure the difficulties, the challenges, the heartaches, and the places of being brokenhearted. It's where you say, "When are these hard days, these cloudy days, going to end?" But then the Lord comes in and makes His presence known and whispers in our spirit, "Hey, there's some sweet cinnamon here as well. This will soothe your brow and comfort your soul. Your days of walking the floor at night are passing."

The third ingredient is two hundred and fifty shekels of sweet-smelling cane, also known as calamus, which is said to stand for order and government. I will define this later. Then the fourth ingredient is five hundred shekels of cassia, which is an equivalent amount to the myrrh. For the moment, I will only say that equivalent amount of five hundred shekels symbolizes worship and praise, which is incredibly important in the light of the suffering. After I've gone through all the other things, my worship at least equals everything I've been through, and I have a praise that is tantamount and comparable to the squeeze I have been in. I deal with this in chapters that follow. All of those four ingredients are mixed together with a hin of oil. In other words, we need something to hold the ingredients together, to bind it together, and then it becomes the anointing oil.

When the priests were consecrated for service, they were anointed with this ointment, the anointing oil. While they may have been anointed on their head, their ear, their thumb, and their big toe, which we considered previously, the anointing oil was primarily put on their garment. So when a priest retired, he would take off the garment and the next priest would put it on, and with it came the fragrance of the anointing oil—which symbolizes the experience and the service of that priest. The next priest doesn't have to start from scratch, but he learns from what the retiring priest has done and gleans from his service. He starts from that point with what is already saturating the garment, and then the anointing carries on.

Now consider that we are part of the priesthood of believers, and if the priest's garment was anointed, that anointing has passed on. The Scripture tell us in Acts 10:38 that God anointed Jesus, and then in 1 John 2:27, it states that we receive the same anointing from Jesus, and it remains in us. That means that we are heavily endowed. By the time it rolls down to us through all those generations, we have what we need in and through Christ to get the job done.

JESUS, THE CRUCIFIED LIFE, AND MYRRH

I want to give you more details about the ingredients in the anointing oil, starting once again with myrrh. Perhaps you feel as though you've had your fill of myrrh from the previous chapter, but there is more instruction to gain. Myrrh is a resin that oozes out of the bark from a small shrub. It's bitter to the taste but has a wonderful fragrance. We saw that it means enduring trials and going through temptations and coming out victorious.

In chapter 3, I also mentioned that the wise men brought gold, frankincense, and myrrh as gifts to Jesus at His birth. I did not mention that at the end of Jesus' life, when He was dying on the cross, "they gave Him wine mingled with myrrh to drink, but he did not take it" (Mark 15:23). It was thought that liquid myrrh, which symbolizes pain, would minimize the pain of the sufferer. Myrrh was also brought at the time that Jesus was entombed, where it was used as a spice along with aloe for His body (John 19:39). So we find myrrh at the beginning and the end of the life of Jesus. That tells me that throughout our lives, we will confront things that are a challenge and a weight to us.

The apostle Paul described how the myrrh worked out in his own life: "I also count all things loss for the excellence of the knowledge of Christ Jesus my Lord, for whom I have suffered the loss of all things, and count them as rubbish, that I may gain Christ and be found in Him, not having my own righteousness, which is from the law, but that which is through faith in Christ, the righteousness which is from God by faith; that I may know Him and the power of His resurrection, and the fellowship of His sufferings, being conformed to His death, if, by any means, I may attain to the resurrection from the dead" (Philippians 3:8–11). Paul is saying, "Lord, I want to know You not just on my good days but the troubled days, not just in the power of Your resurrection but in the fellowship Your sufferings." Rather than run from the suffering, Paul understood that it would work out much better if he entered into the spirit of the suffering that the Lord Jesus Christ had.

And so myrrh becomes a part of what the believer looks to grow from and expects as part of the discipleship training, taking up our cross to follow Jesus (Luke 14:33). It's not always flying high, feeling good, getting deference from other people and blessings, but the true taste of discipleship is the taste of self-denial and sacrifice. After all, the servant is not greater than the Master. Read the John 13 account of Jesus' washing the feet of His disciples. You wouldn't put that at the top of your résumé: "I went to graduate school to wash feet." Having a servant's heart is not given much accord today, and we live in a culture that makes us want to have as much convenience and comfort as possible. But the taste of discipleship is one that removes our pride, and it says, "Lord, whatever I have to go through, I am willing to go through it for You."

Sometimes the way up is a bitter way. Sometimes the way out is a hard way. Sometimes the way through and over begins in an empty pit with no provisions.

After Joseph had been thrown into the pit by his brothers, you can imagine the heartbreak and the disappointment he experienced, knowing his brothers were preparing to kill him. Recall that when the traders came along, and his brothers sold him to them to take into Egypt, the traders were carrying with them several spices, one of which was the bitter myrrh and also balm, a healing ointment (Genesis 37:25). As horrible of a nightmare as this enslavement must have been to Joseph, it eventually led to not only his escape and deliverance, but his elevation and ascension. So sometimes the way up is a bitter way. Sometimes the way out is a hard way. Sometimes the way through and over begins in an empty pit with no provisions. But trouble is never empty-handed. True trouble, the true suffering that the Lord has permitted, is not an empty pit. So look for it. Look for the provision. "God, what have You provided in this tomb I'm in?" Well, in the tomb there was a resurrection!

I want you to get that in your spirit. The apostle Peter said, "But may the God of all grace, who called us to His eternal glory by Christ Jesus, after you have suffered a while, perfect, establish, strengthen, and settle you" (1 Peter 5:10). If you're in a hard place, look for the healing for it. Look for the myrrh in it. Look for the promotion out of it. Peter said there is a time limit on it. There's an expiration date to trouble.

In Isaiah 53:3, we're told that Jesus was "a Man of sorrows and acquainted with grief." It wasn't a passing momentary experience, but He was acquainted with it. He had to go through it. "He was despised, and we did not esteem Him." Long before Jesus was crucified physically, He lived a crucified life. He lived out of the core and center of the divine life of His Father. How do I know that? Because He said, "Whatever I speak, just as the Father told Me, so I speak" (John 12:50). He only did what the Father told Him to do, and He only did His Father's work.

You and I do not have to go to Calvary, but we are invited by the Lord to live a crucified life. That was summed up succinctly when John the Baptist said, "He [Jesus] must increase, but I must decrease" (John 3:30). Jesus was a Man of sorrows, and He mourned for our sinful nature, and yet He was full of joy because of His Father. And that is the mingling, the mixed experience, that Jesus had and we have as believers.

THE ECONOMICAL MOVE OF GOD

In John 7:37–39, it states about the Holy Spirit, "On the last day, that great day of the feast, Jesus stood and cried out, saying, 'If anyone thirsts, let him come to Me and drink. He who believes in Me, as the Scripture has said, out of his heart will flow rivers of living water.' But this He spoke concerning the Spirit, whom those believing in Him would receive; for the Holy Spirit was not yet given, because Jesus was not yet glorified."

It is interesting and perplexing that John would state at that moment in history that "the Holy Spirit was not yet given, because Jesus was not yet glorified." We know from Genesis 1:2 that the Spirit of God was moving over the face of creation, bringing order out of chaos. And John tells us that "in the beginning was the Word [Jesus], and the Word was with God, and the Word was God" (John 1:1). So clearly, the triune God—the Father, Son, and Spirit—was present in and before the beginning of creation, yet Jesus tells us that the Holy Spirit was not yet given that day. How can this be?

To answer this requires that we define what we call an economical move of God. The economy of God means that no matter how situations in our lives look, all things work together for good if I love the Lord and am called according to His purpose (Romans 8:28). That's the rule of how God runs His universe. There's no waste in God—every move of God is intentional, targeted, and part of the divine plan. That means, for instance, that with every temptation, He will make a way of escape. I can count on that in the economy of God. In the economy of God, where there is a demand or a need, the anointing increases to supply that need. We see this repeatedly throughout the ministry of Jesus, the Anointed One. Whenever there was a demand—a sickness, an infirmity, a demon that must be cast out, a hungry crowd—the anointing of God upon Jesus was given in a measure of grace without limit. Nothing is wasted in the economy of God.

My purpose here is to show that in the economy of God, there is nothing static about the Holy Spirit or the anointing. Just as the Holy Spirit moved on creation and moved on people throughout the Old Testament, we see the Spirit operating throughout the life and ministry of Jesus. I am suggesting that there was never a time when the Spirit was not operating along with the Word of the Father and causing all things to work together for good. All things, the good and the bad, serve the purpose.

It happens first in the incarnation, where the Word becomes flesh—and here we reference how the Spirit of God, the anointing of God, worked. Before the birth of Jesus, Mary was told "the Holy Spirit will come upon you, and the power of the Highest will overshadow you" (Luke 1:35) and "that which is conceived in her is of the Holy Spirit" (Matthew 1:20). In theological terms for this miracle, we'd say the economical move of God is that the triune God was unified with tripartite man—body, soul, and spirit.

So the presence of God, the Holy Spirit, is now evident as the Word becomes flesh in a human man, Jesus Christ, and lived a crucified life for thirty-three years. That's part of the economical move of God. We see the Spirit of God as a dove descend upon Jesus when He was baptized in the Jordan (Matthew 3:16), empowering His life and words and deeds. Jesus was fully God and fully man. He lived in His humanity, but He never lived by His humanity. He lived by the divine life of the Spirit in His human life. Eventually, Jesus went to the cross where He "yielded up His spirit" (Matthew 27:50). Finally, the Holy Spirit is stated as having "raised Jesus from the dead" (Romans 8:11).

So let's go back to John 7:39. "This He spoke concerning the Spirit, whom those believing in Him would receive; for the Holy Spirit was not yet given, because Jesus was not yet glorified." Jesus is saying that another change is going to take place. What we have already seen in Jesus is that the power, the presence, and the anointing of God have all flowed as a part of God's plan. There has been a compounding of the Spirit of God with Christ's divinely enriched humanity, His human living by the divine life of His Father (not living according to the flesh), His crucifixion with His all-inclusive judicial redemption (in other words, sin was judged, death was judged, the way of the world was judged, and He won the victory), and His all-surpassing resurrection with its power.

So what am I saying? The language that's used in John 7:39 is that there was a compounding of the Holy Spirit coming. And you are asking, what does this have to do with anything? Well, the instruction that God gave to Moses was to take the ingredients and create a compound, a holy anointing oil. To form a compound means you have combined more than one ingredient and made something totally different. There is a crescendo of the Holy Spirit working from the beginning of time until now.

So for the sake of our understanding—but not in biblical terms—I refer to the compounded Holy Spirit. The Spirit of God was there in the beginning, but that was a phase. When Jesus said that the Holy

The economy of God means that no matter how situations in our lives look, all things work together for good if I love the Lord and am called according to His purpose (Romans 8:28).

Spirit was not yet given, it's not that the Spirit of God was not existing, but there is this increasing, this ascending, this more elaborate, more expanded move of God, so that Jesus becomes the final revelation.

In the Old Testament, we speak of the Spirit of God. Then we speak of the Spirit of Jesus of Nazareth in human form. Then we speak of the Spirit of Christ as being manifested as the risen Lord. After the crucifixion and the resurrection, we use a term that says the pneumatic Christ. That's what Jesus was talking to Nicodemus about in John 3. *Pneuma* is the Greek word for "breath, spirit, or wind." Jesus said you don't know where the Spirit's going to move. He's like the wind; you don't know when He's going to breathe. You don't know when He's going to bring you this way and take you there and change your schedule and alter your plans. The pneumatic wind of God. God is on the loose.

Another example is that in the Old Testament, the Spirit of the Lord moved upon men. In the New Testament, men moved in the power of the Spirit or the power of the resurrected Lord. This clearly evidences a greater manifestation.

What's the summation? The summation is that the anointing flowed through these times, and we end up where we can have the filling and the fullness of the Holy Spirit. Yes, God is on the move! He's moved on us. He's moved in us. He's moved for us. Thus, we don't have the right to say we can't have success, can't get the victory, can't be overcomers, can't be conquerors. There was a time when the Holy Spirit had not been given, but I have a headline for you. I have news for you. *The Holy Spirit has been given!* Holy Spirit power has been provided!

Anytime the enemy tries to tell you, "You don't have the power yet, you don't have the understanding yet, you don't know enough Scripture yet," you should answer, "Wait a minute. The Holy Spirit has been given and poured out as a gift—not earned, not purchased, not bought." Everything that was part of the judicial redemption of God was accomplished. Jesus' redemption included male and female, every nation, and every people, kindred, and tribe that would come and confess His name. The verdict has been rendered that our sins have been forgiven. Yes, He said, "You are My child." We talk about Romans 8:14, "For as many as are led by the Spirit of God,

WE DON'T JUST GO THROUGH SUFFERING,

BUT IT IS MYRRH FOR US,

BRINGING US TO A PLACE OF ANOINTED

SERVICE BECAUSE WE RELATE TO THE

SWEETNESS OF JESUS' DEATH IN THAT

HE WON THE VICTORY.

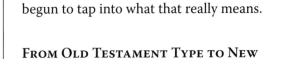

these are the sons of God," but I don't think we've begun to tap into what that really means.

FROM OLD TESTAMENT TYPE TO NEW TESTAMENT REALITY

With calamus, there is a straightness that, even though the soil is miry clay, reflects a strength in our relationship with God.

And so this compound of the anointing oil, which God defined in the book of Exodus, is a type, a shadow, a symbol of the Holy Spirit. In the New Testament, we get definitions and realities concerning the Spirit, but we need to know that this was all a part of God's great divine plan from the very beginning, with the Old Testament pointing to, unfolding, and unveiling who Jesus is. When Jesus was walking with the disciples on the road to Emmaus, He began to explain to them in all the Scriptures, beginning at Moses and all the Prophets, the things concerning Himself (Luke 24). All through every event of biblical history, there was this economical move of God. All of these things were building up like a great drumroll until the point that Jesus came full of the Holy Spirit and power, with the fullness of the Godhead in union with the tripartite man. Isn't that incredible?

So why do we think that we should not benefit from all that has gone before us? The compound anointing is the result of cumulative experiences. We have joined the race or, as I once read, jumped on a moving train with those who preceded us and others who will follow us. We are to evolve and grow. The myrrh is making us. The sweet cinnamon is going to make us. The calamus experiences are going to make us, and we are going to come to new heights of worship.

That's what God has for us. If I have seemingly countless days of myrrh or trouble, and I have just half as much of sweet days of cinnamon, and if I have to deal with some calamus-like order and discipline, it's all right, because all of this is bringing me into fellowship and union with God. He so loved us, not just that He gave His only begotten Son, but that the Holy Spirit of God kept showing up and showing out until the Spirit is referred to us as not just the Spirit of God, not just the Spirit of Jesus, not just the Spirit of Christ, but becomes the Holy Spirit. What is it that God has not done for us?

We are invited to live by faith in Christ in this life. Are you with me? If I live my life by the rule of my own carnal thoughts, it will be a shipwreck. But it has been made possible to say as Paul says, "I have been crucified with Christ; it is no longer I who live, but Christ lives in me; and the life which I now live in the flesh I live by faith in the Son of God, who loved me and gave Himself for me" (Galatians 2:20). So I am to live the anointed life by the power of Jesus Christ in my life, in this life. The Holy Spirit is still operative as Jesus lives His life in me, doing in me what He did in the life of Jesus. As Jesus received the myrrh mingled with wine at the cross, so we go through things and participate in the death of Jesus. We don't just go through suffering, but it is myrrh for us, bringing us to a place of anointed service because we relate to the sweetness of His death in that He won the victory. That's the bitterness of the myrrh in the mouth but the sweet fragrance on the other end.

SWEET-SMELLING CINNAMON AND THE OIL OF GLADNESS

I must move on to the second ingredient of the anointing oil. Sweet-smelling cinnamon comes from the bark of a tree, and it has a sweet fragrance. Because it is a tall stalk, straight and upright, the cinnamon represents integrity. So despite the myrrh—the pain, the misery, the problems in our lives—there is an expectation that we will live a life of integrity, an upright life. As an example of an upright man, read the description of Job in Job 1–2. An anointed life is a walk in truth and a work in truth.

The flower of the cinnamon tree has an offensive smell, but the bark is sweet. It is interesting that the elements of the anointing vary so, which reminds me of the body of Christ and how the different parts works together. If you read Philippians 2:14–16, it speaks to us of how the sweet cinnamon is styled in the life of the believer. "Do *all* things without complaining and disputing, that you that you may become blameless and harmless, children of God without fault in the midst of a crooked and perverse generation, among whom you shine as lights in the world, holding fast the word of life." Do "all" things without murmuring—ouch! Paul is saying, "This is how you ought to live." In other words, everything around us may be adverse and distasteful, but despite what's going on, we are to live a life of purity and sweetness and to shine as lights as Jesus is the light.

Hebrews 1:9 speaks about Jesus, "You have loved righteousness and hated lawlessness; therefore God, Your God, has anointed You with the oil of gladness more than Your companions." This is the uprightness, the purity, the nature of Jesus who suffered from the beginning to the end, who was a Man of sorrows, acquainted with grief, yet loved right doing, right ways, loved integrity and uprightness. You have to fall in love with right in order to do right. Jesus loved righteousness and hated lawlessness.

Do you see that it's not all myrrh? God has anointed Jesus with the oil of gladness. It's saying that this is the sweetness of the nature of the Lord Jesus Christ, and that taste of sweetness, that integrity, will cover a multitude of sins. We have been called and set aside as believers to be those who are not going to be like the smelly flower of the cinnamon that represents the corruptness that is in our culture, but instead we are going to be pleasant and our life is going to give a fragrance of integrity and truth.

CALAMUS AND THE ANOINTING OIL

The third ingredient of the anointing is two hundred and fifty shekels of calamus or sweet-smelling cane. Calamus is a tall reed, so there's that aspect of uprightness again. It also usually grows in a hostile environment of mud and clay that requires strength in growth. It is referred to as a branch, so calamus speaks to us about living in an abiding relationship with the Lord Jesus Christ. Jesus said, "I am the vine, you are the branches" (John 15:5). It's speaking of that kind of mutuality, that kind of connection.

So in order to have the ingredients of the anointing, there are the painful days, but also the sweet fragrance of an upright and pure life. Then with calamus, there is a straightness that, even though the soil is miry clay, reflects a strength in our relationship with God. This is a life of discipline—the disciple's life. This reed, calamus, is considered to be a channel through which things can flow, as a branch does. It speaks of living in a difficult environment, yet despite that there is an intimate relationship with the Lord that is ever-increasing, and it leads to victory. So here it talks about the nurture and the indwelling, the inflowing, the influx that comes from being in a relationship with the Lord.

Perhaps you're in a messy situation, which the Old Testament calls "miry clay." Even though there is the pain, you still love integrity and righteousness. You don't compromise with the hostile environment that's around you. It's not an environment that is conducive to your purpose and what God has called you to. Because you can draw from your relationship with the Lord, you still thrive and the love of Christ flows through your life.

This is beautifully depicted in Psalm 137. The psalmist starts with, "By the rivers of Babylon." "By the rivers" would typically sound like a very promising thing, but this is the river of the enemy, Babylon, that took us captive and away from our Jerusalem. "There we sat down, yea we wept when we remembered Zion." The writer remembered Jerusalem, a place where David danced the dance as he went up the hill to Zion with the ark of the Covenant. Now in this place of the enemy, "we hung our harps upon the willows." We call them weeping willows, and its branches are all bent over. He says, "We just put away the thing that allowed us to make mirth and joy, because our captors required of us a song, saying, 'Sing us one of the songs of Zion! How shall we sing the LORD's song in a foreign land?'"

No matter what is going on in my life, I have the constant companions of goodness and mercy following me. In a hostile place, all I have to do is turn around and see goodness and mercy.

But read on: "If I forget you, O Jerusalem, let my right hand forget its skill! If I do not remember you, let my tongue cling to the roof of my mouth—if I do not exalt Jerusalem above my chief joy." It is saying that even though he is in a murky, miry, awful situation, he has not forgotten how to praise God. He has not forgotten the courts of the Lord. He has not forgotten the presence of the Lord in His temple.

Do you know that you can go through some unspeakable indignities in your life? Despite the environment, God has given us this faith, and the Spirit of the Lord can transport us. David said, "Surely goodness and mercy shall follow me all the days of my life" (Psalm 23:6). No matter what is going on in my life, I have the constant companions of goodness and mercy following me. In a hostile place, all I have to do is turn around and see goodness and mercy. I just need to remind myself of the fruit of Spirit, the peace and love and joy, the nature of Christ, in my life. When the nature of Jesus is formed in me, the anointing can follow. Then the presence of the Lord is there, and this is saying, "Don't forget the relationship, the intimate calamus, the sweetness in a hostile environment that comes from knowing God, the order of God, the sequencing of God, the significance of how He plans out our lives."

Some writers say that calamus stands for the governing order of God, and His governing order is the order of love. And let me tell you what love does. The love of God sandpapers my heart. It is sweet, but it sandpapers my heart so that I understand roughness and coarseness, loss and homelessness and joblessness, and grief and sorrow. The reason love does that for us is so that we can enter into the sufferings of others and have an anointing on our life that doesn't say, "I am your wonder-worker, coming to rescue you," but we will begin to say, "I am pointing to the Lord Jesus Christ," and He can send us and use us. As Bishop Jakes says, "Instead of one Son, we became many sons." The anointing begins to flow and to rush out.

I challenge you to remember Zion for a moment. Remember where you met the Lord. Remember where He saved you. Remember where He called you. Remember when He convicted you. Remember when He spoke to you. Remember when He calmed you. Remember when He healed you. Remember when He spoke your name. It is a place in God. A place of intimate fellowship. A place of exchange. A place where the love of God flows through us as He is the vine and we are the branches. It is an abiding intimate relationship with God, that He is near when you most need Him.

THE ANOINTING FLOWS

When Jesus read Isaiah 61 in the synagogue, He declared that the Spirit of the Lord was upon Him to preach good tidings to the poor, to reach those in need. He was sent to heal the brokenhearted. He was anointed to recover sight to the blind and proclaim liberty to the captives. He was anointed for the opening of the prison to those who are bound. And He was anointed to proclaim the acceptable year of the Lord.

In other words, the anointing is saying, "This is the day. This is the day for change. This is the hour for renewal." It's not just for me to sit in the corner and say, "I'm doing okay." The anointing rises. It flows like tears from that shrub and that tree. It gives the right fragrance. It's a channel in the midst of parched and miry clay and harsh environments. That's what the anointing of God is for. What would we not want to sacrifice and give to the Lord because of His marvelous provision in our lives?

We find myrrh at the beginning and the end of the life of Jesus. That tells me that throughout our lives, we will confront things that are a challenge and a weight to us.

THE WORLD IS PERISHING FOR LACK

OF THE KNOWLEDGE OF GOD,

and the church is famishing for want of His presence.

THE INSTANT CURE OF MOST OF OUR

what a

religious ills would be to enter the presence in spiritual experience, to become suddenly aware that we are in God and that God is in us. This would lift us out of our pitiful narrowness and cause our hearts to be enlarged. . . . What a broad world to roam in, what a sea to swim in is this God and Father of our Lord Jesus Christ.

A. W. TOZER

sea to swim

CHAPTER EIGHT

GET IN POSITION

"Behold,

I send the Promise of My Father upon you;

but tarry in the city of Jerusalem

until you are endued with power

from on high."

LUKE 24:49

hile I wish this didn't have to be repeated, I find it necessary to always reemphasize in my teaching that the anointing of the Holy Spirit is for service. The anointing is not somehow to put us in a position to be looked up to or to have a string of impressive titles and labels handed to us. The anointing is not for pumping us up or for bragging or making us the star of the show. When the Lord gave the instruction to Moses regarding the anointing oil, He said, "It shall not be poured on man's flesh" (Exodus 30:32). It's not to somehow bring out our best personality or to draw attention to us and our gifts—the anointing is for service.

It is also important to remind ourselves from Psalm 133 that the precious anointing oil that went on Aaron's head flows in only one direction—down. That being the case, the greatest impact, the greatest momentum is at the bottom. That's the place to be. It has come down through the generations and the ages. It comes down to what we sometimes look at as hierarchical structures. No wonder Jesus could look down through the ages and say, "Greater works than these he will do" (John 14:12). Consider all the advantages that we have to do the work and the ministry of the Lord today as the Holy Spirit has been poured out and compounded for greater works in so many ways.

We want to be in the current of the flow of the anointing. It's so easy to move away from the flow, getting caught up with who we are and thinking more highly of ourselves than we should and demanding more than we should. We are part of the body of Christ, a hand or a foot, and as the anointing flows down from Him, if we've somehow gotten ourselves disconnected and disjointed, we will not be covered with the anointing oil, the presence of the Lord, the empowerment of God. Some will be uninvolved and suffer atrophy, as happens to an arm or a leg that's not being used, and others will be overused and overworked. But when our alignment is right, the anointing can come from the head to the entire body. So we don't want to be in the counterflow; we want to be anointed for service.

The Father's anointing is for the entire body of Christ. He intends for every believer to be anointed and empowered. Jesus told His disciples, "Behold, I send the Promise of My Father upon you; but tarry in the city of Jerusalem until you are endued with power from on high" (Luke 24:49). *Endued* means to "be clothed on, to put on" the power that you need for ministry and for service, which may be in your home, on your job, in your church, or wherever God places you.

Endued also means to "slip comfortably into a garment." Jesus is saying, "You need power to be able to wear the robe of righteousness I have provided for you. You need power to be able to withstand and go through all the things the enemy is hurling at you. You need the power of God, and you can't afford to have the garments of salvation not fitting well. You need to be suited comfortably to do the service of God." Clearly, the Lord intends for His bride, for the body of Christ, to not be empty-handed, to not to be weaponless, but to be anointed from on high.

THE EXCEEDING GREATNESS OF HIS POWER

When the apostle Paul talks about the Father's anointing, he states, "and what is the exceeding greatness of His power toward us who believe, according to the working of His mighty power" (Ephesians 1:19). You need to spend a month meditating on that word alone. In other words, the exceeding great God goes beyond what He has already done. Whatever boundaries, whatever marks have been done in the past, God is exceeding in His greatness. God is always doing more and bigger and greater and higher than what He last did. Can you fathom that in your spirit?

The anointing builds this expectation in us over time, not just because "He did it before, He can do it again," but because He can do exceedingly abundantly above all that I'm even able to ask or think. Now if we can begin to get a sense of the magnitude, just a little bit of understanding of what God wants to do in our lives, He's saying it is exceedingly great. God is excelling and overriding whatever has been done, and He has no competition. There is no one beside Him, no one like Him, and no one can save like our God.

Remember that whatever God says about Himself in His Word is forever settled. There's no one rivaling it, no one pulling it up, no one editing it, no one who's copyrighting it—it is the unchanging Word of God. God sets His own record forth: "I Am Who I Am. I'm not just who I was yesterday, even though I'm immutable and I do not change. But I Am Who I Am for you today, and I Am here for you tomorrow." That is the God whom we serve—exceeding, exceeding, exceeding greatness!

Based upon His Word, I'm compelled to look at my own life and the church and say, "If God has provided this exceeding great power toward us, what am I, or we, missing? What am I, or we, not doing? Is there evidence in my life and in the church of the exceeding greatness and the power of God operating?" Perhaps we need to ask the Lord to help us be in right alignment, to be in the right position to be properly covered with His anointing. We need Him to help us get in the right direction of the flow and the anointing that's coming down so we can be used of God. He's promised power to us in His Holy Spirit, and we are the members of His body, seeking

Whatever boundaries, whatever marks have been done in the past, God is exceeding in His greatness. God is always doing more and bigger and greater and higher than what He last did.

to be rightly connected, and thus it is rightfully ours by virtue of all that Jesus had done and provided for us.

We are reminded in 2 Corinthians 4:7 that "we have this treasure [this valuable costly anointing of God] in earthen vessels, that the excellence of the power may be of God and not of us." That's where we need to get. What we need to recognize and say is, "The power is not of us. It's not about who we are. It's not about what we think we can do, because it's all about God."

Indeed, Jesus is the center of all that we're doing. So we receive gifting from the Lord to position us rightly under spiritual fathers and spiritual mothers to do the work of God, and the anointing flows and we learn how to go in the direction and with the current of the flow. The apostle Peter says, "Submit yourselves to your elders. Yes, all of you be submissive to one another, and be clothed with humility, for 'God resists the proud, but gives grace to the humble'" (1 Peter 5:5). We are to humble ourselves under the mighty hand of God and learn from the anointed among us.

THE DIVINE APOTHECARY

I want to focus once again on the anointing oil: "And thou shalt make it an oil of holy ointment, an ointment compound after the art of the apothecary: it shall be an holy anointing oil" (Exodus 30:25 KJV). He is saying to make the holy anointing oil after "the art of the apothecary." In other words, don't just make it as Grandma said, "Add a pinch of this or that." He said no, there's an exact plan for this. There's a purpose to the ingredients that brings the anointing in your life, and it's not for us or someone else to determine what those ingredients are. We saw previously that being like Jesus was like the olive that was in Gethsemane and through the suffering of death had the anointing oil symbolically pressed out of His life. The making of the anointing by the art of the divine Apothecary, the Chemist, the great Pharmacist of our lives may be crafted to come through rejection, heartache, separation, divorce, X-rays that are frightening, or through our finances sifting away. But it's all the making of the anointing in our lives, even though it may look nothing like the script we would write for ourselves.

Our Pharmacist is the one who says that all things work together for the good of them that love the Lord and are called according to His purpose. He says, "Don't just throw anything together and call yourself into My priest-hood. Don't just go into your backroom and put together a line or two because it sounded good to you, but follow My prescription." Live your life as designed by the master Craftsman. There is not only a balm in Gilead, but there is a Chief Physician. There is a divine Chemist. There is a Pharmacist who knows how to bring together the elements in our lives so that we are fit and suited for the service of God. This too is evidence of compounding in our lives.

In the art of the apothecary, the pharmacist would crush the herbs to make the medicinal elements, and he typically relied on liquid, and thus used liquid measures. My question of the text in Exodus 30:25 is, if they're making a "holy ointment," why is it called "a holy anointing oil" in the last of the phrase? Why does it go from ointment to anointing oil? Here's why. Ointment is in a settled state, but anointing means there is action, a flow. So to be anointed is not to sit around and look spiritual and saintly or to stand and look holy and sanctimonious. I don't have an anointing on my life so I can be religious. The ointment was made for the anointing, the action and the flowing. It's meant to be passed on.

And because it's anointing oil, it means it can be poured. So the Lord is pouring out. Pentecost, we're told, was the fulfillment of the prophecy of Joel: "In the last days, God says, I will pour out my Spirit on all people" (Acts 2:17). He is saying, "I will open up the windows of heaven and pour out an anointing that is far more than you have room to receive. I am not going to drop, throw, or release it on you. No, I'm going to pour it on you." When something is pouring on, and I'm in proper alignment, it can't rain on my head and miss my shoulders or elbows. When I line up, and I'm in the flow of what God is doing, He provides a downpour from heaven that soaks all of me.

The cloud of God's glory will unzip and release the rain of His Spirit. That's what God wants for us. That's the Father's anointing. I don't know about you, but I don't want just a drop. I want the Spirit of God to move mightily in my life, so I have to fall on my face and cover up my face, because His glory can just seem like a bit too much. It's not good enough just to have the ointment. I want the pouring out of the anointing!

OUR PHARMACIST IS THE ONE

WHO SAYS THAT ALL THINGS WORK

TOGETHER FOR THE GOOD OF THEM

THAT LOVE THE LORD AND ARE CALLED

ACCORDING TO HIS PURPOSE.

Remember that the garment worn by the priest would capture the precious anointing oil. That tells me I don't need a new vision for the church. I don't need a competitive plan or an alternative purpose. I am to capture the anointing that's in the garment of the head of the church. You have to capture the anointing because it's there. So we are catching it, and we are slipping into the garment, and we are wearing Elijah's garment even though we are Elisha, and the world is standing up and witnessing to the fact and asking, "Oh, where is the Lord God of Elijah?" He's with Elisha now, and that anointing is in you and with you and for you, making it possible for you to do and to be all that God has said.

THE LIVING WATER THAT FLOWS

Clearly, the ointment must become an anointing. It must be in service. It must be busy. It reminds me of the story of the widow of a prophet in 2 Kings 4. When the creditors were coming to take her sons because she had no money to pay her debt, God gave her a plan through the prophet Elisha. She was told to borrow as many empty vessels as she could, and "do not gather just a few." But just gathering and sitting the empty borrowed vessels around the house did not do the job. What she had to do was take the tiny bit of oil that was left in her house, and she had to pour it out. I'm suggesting to you that what you have, pour it out. Don't hold on to it; release it. Pour it out.

So the woman had to pour it out, and as she poured, she filled all the vessels, until there were no vessels left. She filled everything, but it wasn't in the borrowing of vessels; it was in the pouring of the oil. It was in going from the ointment to the anointing. We have to take the anointing and pour it out in the real world. In her obedience to the prophet's instruction, she shared in the subsequent obedience of Jesus Christ, and the anointing flowed like a river, with her in its stream.

Then there was the wedding at Canaan that we considered in the Introduction, where they were out of wine and the ruler of the feast didn't realize it. There were six big stone pots that were sitting there, representing the old law, the traditions, and the old Jewish way, which the Bible says were empty. Jesus said to fill the pots with water, and then to pour it out. It was when they began to pour it out that the confession was made by the ruler of the feast that this was the best wine. I see in this that my old ways are empty. My old traditions are empty. The new wine of the Spirit poured out is better than my traditions. This is better than "I've always done it this way." This is better than "this is the way I learned it."

There's also the better water that Jesus talked to the Samaritan woman about at the well—"the water that I shall give him will never thirst again. But the water that I shall give him will become in him a fountain of water springing up into everlasting life" (John 4:13). The woman said, "Our fathers worshiped on this mountain." The new way is better, because through Jesus we "worship in spirit and truth . . . for the Father is seeking such to worship Him." There's really no comparison to how much better that is. His presence is not conformed to a particular church building, but the worshiper is invited to meet the presence of God in Christ.

Consider also the water that was at the pool of Bethesda where the man who had the infirmity for thirty-eight years could not get into the pool fast enough when an angel occasionally would stir the water (John 5). The manifestations of the old Jewish system were sporadic. Sometimes you saw it, sometimes you didn't, but with the Spirit outpoured through Jesus, the Anointed One, there was no waiting. It wasn't a maybe or maybe not that the angel would stir, but it was a consistent anointing and an outpouring through Jesus—a constant on the Lord's part to bless us.

This is the fresh move of God! This is the working of God. This is the new dispensation of the grace of God. This is the virtue of Jesus Christ. This is the fruit of the Spirit—the love, joy, peace, longsuffering, kindness, goodness, faithfulness, gentleness, and self-control (Galatians 5:22–23). That's what we need. I can't just be anointed and not have the attractive virtues of Christ's character. I need the nature of Christ in order to maintain that anointing on my life.

Remember that the Holy Spirit is "the living water" that Jesus said would flow out of our hearts (John 7:38–39). In Ezekiel 47, He is the water flowing out of the temple, which symbolizes Jesus, that brings healing wherever it goes throughout the world. You're in that river, and the river is rising, and you can swim in it. That's the water that Jesus said He would give to the

Samaritan woman and she would never thirst again. That is the water we need!

Paul says, "Do you not know that your body is the temple of the Holy Spirit who is in you?" (1 Corinthians 6:19). When you accept Christ into your life, you are a temple, and in you is the living flow of the Holy Spirit. You have the living waters that made the wine in Canaan. You have the living waters that healed the man in the pool of Bethesda. You have the living waters that cause you to never thirst again. You have the dew of Hermon that starts descending the mountains of Zion and becomes the Jordan River (Psalm 133).

Never believe the enemy's lies that you are defeated or a failure. You are significant in the plan of God. You are on the top and not the bottom. You are the head and not the tail. You are above and not beneath, because living waters flow in and out of your temple. You are anointed!

THE SENT ONE HAS COME

Shortly before Jesus went to the cross, He spent a lot of His final hours preparing His disciples for what would happen when He was gone. One of the promises He gave them when they were sorrowful about the news of His departure was, "Nevertheless I tell you the truth. It is to your advantage that I go away; for if I do not go away, the Helper will not come to you; but if I depart, I will send Him to you. . . . I still have many things to say to you, but you cannot bear them now. However, when He, the Spirit of truth, has come, He will guide you into all truth" (John 16:7, 12–13). This promise of the anointing is ours as well.

The new wine of the Spirit poured out is better than my traditions. This is better than "I've always done it this way." This is better than "this is the way I learned it."

He was saying to those who believed in Him that He would send the Holy Spirit to give them this further understanding of all that He had taught them, and it would come through the anointing, the presence of God. They didn't have the fullness yet, but not to worry. The Holy Spirit was coming to teach them all the things that Jesus wanted them to know, to guide them into all truth. And the Spirit's presence in their lives was actually to their advantage over Jesus being physically present with them. They had no idea of the depth of understanding and the fullness of revelation that was coming their way through the anointing.

You and I need to have a constant expectation in God of what the Holy Spirit is moving on in our lives. I'm expecting to see things that my eyes have not seen before. I'm expecting to hear things that my ears have not heard before. I'm expecting to receive and participate in a joy and in a fullness that I cannot describe. "Eye has not seen, nor ear heard, nor have entered into the heart of man the things which God has prepared for those who love Him" (1 Corinthians 2:9).

Yes, that's the expectation I have, because my God is not limited to an angel's sporadic stirrings of the water in the one pool of Bethesda. My God is not stuck in some unused, unequipped, unemployed, inactive mode of empty water pots at a wedding. My God is busy pouring water and making wine. My God is active. He's always on the move, helping and caring and forgiving and loving and healing and fixing and lifting.

Now I know Him as the Healer. Now I know Him as the Keeper. Now I know Him as the Savior. Now I know Him as the Redeemer. He's brought me a long way. He has walked with me down lonely roads. He's the one who dries my tears. He's the one who picks me up and is the glory and the lifter of my head. And I'm looking farther down the road and pressing on to meet Him. I'm going after what God has. I'm pursuing and chasing, and He's drawing me into more and more, deeper and deeper in the living water.

Because God is doing that, I desire to participate in the same way. He has called us to be caregivers, lifters, servers, and builders. He's called us to be involved, to be engaged in the world. What was attractive about Jesus was that He was living the divine life, pouring it out. What's attractive about us is when we're living the Christ life, pouring it out. It attracts other people to know who the Savior is, but also our anointing is drawn to the problems and where the need is.

Are you getting a taste and a hunger for more of God? Are you desiring a fresh touch from the Lord? The flowing of the Holy Spirit is not just when you're in church listening to a moving sermon or in worship. The anointing should be in your car and your home, at your breakfast and dinner table, in difficult and glorious circumstances. The anointing is to be yours at this very moment. By faith receive the gift of God's presence now!

What was attractive about Jesus was that
He was living the divine life, pouring it out.
What's attractive about us is when we're living
the Christ life, pouring it out.

WORSHIP OF OUR GOD IS OUR HIGHEST CALLING,

our deepest walk, and our greatest joy.

Worship bring.

WORSHIP BRINGS INTIMACY WITH GOD.

T. D. JAKES

CHAPTER NINE

WORSHIP AS DIALOGUE

"The hour is coming, and now is,

when the true worshipers will worship

the Father in spirit and truth;

for the Father is seeking such to worship Him.

God is Spirit,

and those who worship Him

must worship in spirit and truth."

JOHN 4:23–24

While I've given considerable attention to three of the four ingredients to the holy anointing oil (the myrrh, sweet cinnamon, and sweet calamus) as described in the instructions the Lord gave to Moses in Exodus 30:22–25, now I want to focus on the fourth ingredient, the five hundred shekels of cassia. Cassia is found in the bark of a shrub that has a beautiful purple flower and tends to grow in high altitudes. Because the biblical root word for *cassia* means "to shrivel down and to bow," it speaks to us of worship, where we submit ourselves and open ourselves up to the will and the Word of the Lord Jesus Christ.

In the life application of what we have studied previously, as we go through the troubles and sufferings of myrrh, we are called to have the purity of sweet cinnamon and the integrity of calamus, which brings us to worship. It instructs us that all of the things we've gone though and are going through give us a reason to pay homage and praise and adoration to God. All that we go through as part of the anointing is taking us through a process so that God can get the glory. And we noted previously that cassia is proportionally the equivalent amount to the myrrh within the anointing oil. That tells us that our worship should be proportionate to our trials. We have a praise that is tantamount and comparable to the difficulties and sufferings we've gone through.

It is interesting that the first time the word *worship* is used in the Bible is on the occasion when Abraham was told to offer Isaac on the altar as a sacrifice. That suggests that worship is an invitation that leads us through the suffering to a place of total surrender and worship. There may be many areas in our lives that we want to cling to, and the Lord is saying surrender. Worship is a willingness to surrender to the Lord.

To Worship Is to Host the Presence of God

Unfortunately, there are all kinds of definitions and disagreements today over what worship is and how to worship, and they regard both within the church and within our personal lives. My purpose is not to address those. There are so many ways to approach the very broad theme of worship. We can approach it culturally, socially, ethically, and theologically, as well as in terms of ritual and tradition and corporate and personal worship. However, we can all agree with the fact that worship is fundamental to the life of every church and to the life of every believer. And while we tend to think of worship as the praise we express through song and prayer, whether in a scripted way from the stage in church or more spontaneously in our personal quiet times, worship includes all that we do to honor the Lord. It is not just our singing, not just the bowing of our heads and hearts in prayer, but includes the reading of Scripture, the Lord's communion table, and in truth all of our obedience and service to the Lord. "And whatever you do, do it heartily, as to the Lord and not to men" (Colossians 3:23).

Worship is an active experience we enter into, not just a lofty thought or theological concept, and it is also a state of being. *It is in worship that we host, or entertain, the presence of God.* The presence whom we are inviting is our loving Father, our Creator and Sustainer, the Almighty God, the great I Am. Through worship, we host His presence, and it becomes a communication, a conversation, a dialogue, where change occurs in our lives. In worship, God draws us to Himself and does so by making a covenant with us and making us His own people. Yes, worship certainly involves paying homage to God for all that He has done in providing for our salvation. But worship, whether through prayer or the communion table or the reading of the Word or times of corporate praise, is the means to help us to enter into the actual experience of the presence of God. This intimate relationship goes beyond covenant and traditions, and at times we are lost in His presence.

Worship has so many aspects and layers to it, and I don't mean to minimize their importance. Sometimes we use the word *liturgy* interchangeably with *worship*. Liturgy tends to speak of the historical church and a body of people who have shared beliefs and expressions that are meaningful to them. The accepted wisdom of the historical church has been that we have a duty and a delight to praise and serve God. Thus, over the course of time, people have found language and procedures and songs and scriptures and readings that they feel brings them into a closer communion with the Lord, and that becomes their custom or their liturgy.

While we tend to think of that expression as being through singing songs and praying together, the liturgy really incorporates everything that we do when we gather and assemble as the body of Christ. For instance, lit candles often are meant to remind us that Jesus is "the light of the world." A standing choir adorned in beautiful robes is intended to remind us of the gathering of the saints around the throne of God. Art and drama are meant to serve in worship as lifting up who God is. Our reading of the Scripture, our taking of what some call the elements of communion and others call the sacraments, our joining in corporate worship together—all of these things mean more than just what they are in the natural. For instance, the unleavened bread and the cup of the communion table draw us into the experience of the death and the burial and the resurrection of Jesus. It's sacramental. It's speaking volumes to our faith.

Worship is an active experience we enter into, not just a lofty thought or theological concept, and it is also a state of being. It is in worship that we host, or entertain, the presence of God.

I believe that the more opportunities that we have that help us to have a participating worship are wonderful. But it is important that we not get so focused on the particular form and style or so stuck in our ritual or tradition that the purpose gets lost. It is not about the form; the form can change. It's not about the style of sanctuary, or whether we have a choir or a worship team, or whether the service is traditional or contemporary. It is about the bringing to mind what God has done, and seeing that in our liturgy and in our elements of worship. It is about the fact that form is an invitation to come and partner with God. The goal is to lead us to experience the presence of the Lord and to sense that He is moving among us. We want to join the prophet Isaiah and see "the Lord sitting on a throne, high and lifted up, and the train of His robe filled the temple" (Isaiah 6:1). In worship, whatever the form or style, we are seeking that His presence invades and pervades in our lives.

Recently, I had a new way of envisioning Isaiah 6. I imagined the "train" not only as the healing in the hem of His garment but the anointing in the veil of His mantle. This imagery spoke volumes to my faith, and it was the first time I had ever associated the "train" with a veil. This is particularly significant to my understanding, because it is as if the veil from the temple now cloaks His majesty. Where once the veil emphasized the exclusiveness of the Holy of Holies, it now manifests the glory of Him who is offered to the nations. It makes me recall the song, "Oh, the glory of Your presence, we your temple give you reverence."

FROM PRECEPT TO PRACTICE

I recently asked Jamar Jones, the Executive Director of the Fine Arts Program at the Potter's House, about how this works out practically in the liturgy of the church. While the form of worship at the Potter's House may be very different from the form utilized in your church, I think you'll find some of the principles as foundational. He told me, "There is a purpose that worship in our churches has of drawing people out of our communities (that's evangelism), who become the crowd who hear the Good News, who embrace the gospel and become the church, who become the committed core, and then it kind of repeats itself. We use music and arts as a tool to draw people in. That's where the transformation starts to happen. People come in weighted with burdens (myrrh), but in and through the anointed worship, their heaviness is transformed to a praise of the faithfulness of God—through it all.

"The attraction must always be Jesus. It's how we're going to present Jesus—centered and governed on the facts of His birth, His life, His death, His resurrection, and the reality that one day He is coming back. The music has to be anointed—it must be the right music and the right sensitivities and discernment of the Holy Spirit to reach the people. The anointing of the Holy Spirit needs to be poured on the vessels who are leading and producing the music. If you have vessels who are not anointed, you will have worship that is not anointed. You can have very skilled musicians and singers, but there will be no transforming connection without the anointing of the Spirit, the presence of God."

WORSHIP IS OUR RESPONSE TO HIS PRESENCE

The cassia of the anointing oil brings with it the sense of reverence. *Worship* is a word that was used when Abraham's servant found a suitable bride for Abraham's son Isaac. The servant was so overwhelmed by the incredible answer to his prayer that it says he "worshiped the LORD, bowing himself to the earth" (Genesis 24:52). There are certain aspects about worship that spontaneously issue from us when we realize that God is working for us and in us and through us.

Part of what we are talking about regarding worship is that we come to know that there is more than who we are, more than what we can see, and more than what we can understand. In worship, the individual goes beyond himself or herself and reaches out to the tremendous mystery of such a marvelous God. The apostle Paul said it this way: "And without controversy great is the mystery of godliness: God was manifested in the flesh, justified in the Spirit, seen by angels, preached among the Gentiles, believed on in the world, received up in glory" (1 Timothy 3:16).

I like to think of worship in practical terms such as, I'm falling into the lap of a God who knows more than my doctors. It is a mystery to me how God can heal with a word, and it leads me to worship Him. It's a mystery how a scripture from His Word can enter into my soul and inspire faith that becomes the foundation for every aspect of my life. Worship is reaching into an area that's beyond our understanding and comprehension.

Worship, as symbolized in the anointing oil by cassia that grows at higher elevations, is a lifting and a going higher. When we worship the Lord, we get beyond what we can see, and touch, and hear, and we are drawn into His presence. In worship, we see God as the initiator, not us, who is seeking us. We didn't decide to seek Him. Our worship is a response to the God who loved us first and sent His Son and Spirit to find us. I seek and pursue Him because He pursued me. He invited me to ask and to seek and to knock. Our worship is a response to our gracious God and Savior.

Consequently, to truly enter into worship or the presence of the Lord, we too seek to be endowed (or clothed) with the covering, anointing oil. We need His presence to cover us so that we can stand in His presence. One hymn says, ". . . dressed in His righteousness alone, faultless to stand before the throne." Clearly, we're not faultless, but the anointing presence of the Holy Spirit of God equips and empowers us to come boldly before the throne of grace in prayer and worship. As the older saints used to say when I was a child, "Bless God's High Name!"

We know that as we worship and come to know the Lord, God is a self-communicating God, a self-revealing God. Only He can really reveal who He is. God has to tell us about who He is, because only He really knows, and He has provided that in His Word. What we discover in His Word is that He is the self-giving God, who calls us to know Him and to have fellowship with Him. And whether we are talking about the Father, Son, or the Holy Spirit, the Triune God, we find that God is God. That's why we say, "God is very God," and His existence is the ground of being. Anywhere we begin to taste and see that the Lord is good, it's still all God, and He is worthy of worship.

When we begin to think about God, His self-giving and self-communicating, through and through being all God, then we begin to say, "Oh, I have to bow as the cassia flower. I have to shrivel. I have to decrease so that God can increase in my life." Then we don't have to be petitioned or instructed to pray or to kneel or to lift or wave our hands. There's something about the presence of God that begins to call, deep unto deep, and draws us out

THERE ARE CERTAIN ASPECTS

ABOUT WORSHIP THAT SPONTANEOUSLY

ISSUE FROM US WHEN WE REALIZE

THAT GOD IS WORKING FOR US

AND IN US AND THROUGH US.

of ourselves and into a place where we don't necessarily have an explanation for how it is that we honor God. But this is our God, the God who takes us from birth and leads us and guides us even unto death. This infinitely beautiful God whom we serve is personal. He knows and loves me and invites me to "enter into His gates with thanksgiving, and into His courts with praise. Be thankful to Him, and bless his name" (Psalm 100:4).

WORSHIP IN SPIRIT AND TRUTH

When people get into disagreements over what worship is and how to worship, whether within church or within our personal lives, it reminds me of the Samaritan woman at the well whom we considered previously. She said to Jesus, "Our fathers worshiped on this mountain, and you Jews say that in Jerusalem is the place where one ought to worship" (John 4:20). The Samaritans had their own temple and their own distorted form of the worship of the God of Israel. But the Lord replied that what the Father wants is those who would worship "in spirit and truth." So we must make sure that we worship God in a way that lines up and is consistent with what God says in His Word.

It has been stated that man's chief end is to glorify God and to enjoy Him forever, and I agree with that. But how many people try to glorify God but never enjoy Him? Believers are encouraged to glorify and obey God, and yet in the lives of so many believers, God remains in some far-off place where there's no way that they can enjoy who God is. I'm talking about not just enjoying the blessings of God, but actually knowing and enjoying Him, the very

When we worship the Lord, we get beyond what we can see, and touch, and hear, and we are drawn into His presence.

presence of God. It is offered that anointed worship is the place of enjoying the Lord.

When asked the question, "Why did God create man in the first place?" some say that it's because God wanted fellowship. Perhaps that's a very limited response if it suggests that God is sitting all alone somewhere over the circle of the earth, and He is so lonely that He just needs to hear my voice. But through creation God breathed into man "the breath of life" so that Adam became a living soul made in the image and likeness of the Creator (Genesis 1:27). He created man and woman to love Him and enjoy fellowship with Him and to rule over His creation, to have dominion. Because we were in Adam, we also were invited into this highest station of authority.

But Adam and Eve, and we with them, lost that position in the Garden through the serpent's conniving and deceit. We see the break in the relationship when Adam and Eve recognized that they were unclothed. They realized that they didn't have any cover, and the Lord came to them and asked them, "Who told you that you were naked?" (Genesis 3:11). Adam gave up that authority and dominion, but God stepped in and sacrificed an animal, took its skin, and made clothing for them. He covered them, and mankind was introduced to the principle called *substitution*. Something had to die so that Adam could live, and that happened through the life of the innocent animal that died in his stead. What they had lost was restored through the sacrifice that pointed to the coming sacrifice of the Lamb of God. Because of the coming and the obedience of the second Adam, Jesus Christ, He became the sacrifice that brings us back into this place of fellowship and dialogue and authority with God.

What does that have to do with worship? It tells us what God requires of us. When we read in Genesis 4 about the sons of Adam and Eve, Cain and Abel, they knew very well what God required of them. They knew that they were supposed to bring a sacrifice in obedience and present their worship to the Lord. And so, in the sacrifice of the killing of the animal, the shedding of blood, there was an offering made. There was worship given to God.

I am suggesting to you that we have the restored authority to speak boldly to the enemy and say, "All the things that you try to accuse me of not having or not being, because of the shedding of blood and the sacrifice of Jesus, I am no longer unclothed. I am no longer exposed. I am no longer a victim. But because of the blood that has been shed on Calvary, there is a covering for me." What is the covering? The covering is that God has given us a new garment of righteousness. And He has given us a garment of praise that was purchased by the blood of Jesus that I might come before Him in a sacrifice of praise and bless His holy name.

POWER IN THE PLACE OF ANOINTED WORSHIP

Cassia then represents my willingness to be conformed to the obedience of Christ that I might be covered by His anointing and enter into the joy (worship) of the Lord. The joy, however, is only partial, because life is full of troubles. We believe that one day our joy will be full and complete. We look for the final consummation of all things in Christ at His return and a day of unspeakable joy.

I love the scripture, "For all the promises of God in [Christ] are Yes, and in Him Amen, to the glory of God through us" (2 Corinthians 1:20). Throughout the Old Testament, we see God looking for those who would be His people, His family, His chosen ones, His worshipers, who would say yes to the will and purpose of God. The reality was that those who claimed to be the people of God often were a huge disappointment. They would be obedient for a while and then fail, until the perfect Man came, the Man of Nazareth, the Word who was made flesh (John 1:14). Remember that God is always giving Himself away, and still there is no less God left behind after the giveaway. God the Father brought forth His Son, the Man of Nazareth, the God who stepped into humanity, and gave a radical yes to everything that God had said. So God found in Jesus the perfect Man, the perfect Son who had the full measure of grace to handle all things and to live a sinless life, to walk with integrity in the midst of a perverse generation, and because Christ said yes to God, now all the promises of God in Him are Yes and Amen.

Although we have failed to say yes on our own to what God has planned and promised, because Jesus has said a radical yes and we have been joined to Jesus, we can say yes today. Through Him, we can receive all that He has promised, because His radical yes has made room and incorporated us. So when the Lord says you can go through and endure hardness as a good soldier, you say, "Yes, I can." That is not because we are so suited to go through it, but it is because Jesus has said yes and we are hidden in Him. When He says, "You are more than a conqueror," it's not that we feel that we are more than a conqueror, but because the perfect Man of Nazareth with the full measure of grace has said that He would conquer and cause us to triumph. These are the things that cause us to worship. All that He has done should constantly strike our hearts with awe and wonder.

When we talk about worship, we are talking about the vocation of communion with God, making it a lifestyle, not just us coming to God with our supplications and our requests, but also listening and hearing and having that pouring out and that pouring in of the Lord in our lives. "God, who at various times and in various ways spoke in time past to the fathers by the prophets, has in these last days spoken to us by His Son" (Hebrews 1:1–2). God has spoken to us through His Son, He is speaking to us today, and God listens to our words and our spirits as well when we call upon Him. When our worship is anointed, it is contagious and is said to infect others with our sense of faith and joy.

So the language of worship often begins with adoration. It begins with acknowledging that God is higher, beyond, above and transcendent, and not beneath. We are limited, because we try to use our human language to adore God, but there is the sense that when we really become immersed in worship and adoration that we connect with an eternal worship that has never stopped. Even the heavens declare His glory. We get a sense of what was experienced and described when the prophet Isaiah tapped into the response of the angels to the presence of God, "Holy, holy, holy!" (Isaiah 6). There is a point at which we don't follow the lines in the song necessarily, where we don't have to think about the next thing we want to say to God or the next line that's coming. It's where the inner man begins to dictate to the outer man, and the melody and lyrics may change. It may be articulate or inarticulate. It may be moans or groans. It may be worship in tears or worship in laughter. It may be an exultant song or sheer silence. There is power in this place of anointed worship. There is power to save, heal, and deliver, because the anointed presence of Christ takes over.

Cassia represents my willingness to be conformed to the obedience of Christ that I might be covered by His anointing and enter into the joy (worship) of the Lord.

What marks genuine worship is that it involves an exchange between us and God in which we enter into a dialogue. In worship, we give of ourselves to God, and He gives of Himself. For our part, the psalmist said, "What shall I render to the LORD for all His benefits toward me?" (Psalm 116:12). The psalmist didn't want to give to God that which cost him nothing. We ought to put something into our worship and praise. You see what's happening in worship is that God is requiring something of us, and what He requires is that we give Him what we have in a tangible way so He can give us those intangible things that we need. So what can I give or render to God? I can give God my undivided time, because my time is valuable, and I can pray, whether I feel like it or not. I can bring a sacrifice of praise through a time of great difficulty.

And when we render to God our worship, He says, "Let Me give you something in exchange," because the God whom we serve is the King of kings and always out gives anyone who's giving to Him. So what God does is to share His benefits with us. He says, "Let me tell you about My healthcare plan. Here is a list of My provisions for you." When we make ourselves available to God, perhaps through prayer and fasting, we are moving ourselves so that we can line up with the body of Christ, so we align ourselves with the anointing that's flowing from Jesus as the Head. We are bringing ourselves to a place voluntarily where we can hear and receive better from the Lord. Our attitude is changed. Our conversation and our recreation are changed. We can walk away from the television or sporting event and get into the Word and pray. By giving God our time and ourselves, we move ourselves in line with the will of God. We are not changing God's plan. We are not trying to bribe or impress God. We're simply putting ourselves in a place to access the anointing of God.

There is power in this place of anointed worship. There is power to save, heal, and deliver, because the anointed presence of Christ takes over.

WITHOUT THE PRESENCE OF THE SPIRIT

there is no conviction, no regeneration,

no sanctification, no cleansing, no acceptable works.

WE CAN PERFORM DUTIES WITHOUT HIM

Life is in the

BUT OUR SERVICE IS DULL AND MECHANICAL.

LIFE IS IN THE QUICKENING SPIRIT.

W. A. CRISWELL

CHAPTER TEN

WORSHIP HIS PRESENCE

It came to pass, when the trumpeters and singers

were as one, to make one sound to be heard in praising

and thanking the LORD, and when they lifted up

their voice with the trumpets and cymbals and

instruments of music, and praised the LORD, saying:

"For He is good, for His mercy endures forever,"

that the house, the house of the LORD,

was filled with a cloud, so that the priests could not

continue ministering because of the cloud;

for the glory of the LORD filled the house of God.

2 CHRONICLES 5:13–14

n the previous chapter, we focused on cassia, the fourth ingredient that God gave to Moses for making the holy anointing oil (Exodus 30:22–25), and I will continue to expand on it here. Cassia is found in the bark of a shrub that grows in high altitudes and possesses a little purple flower. Biblically, *cassia* means "to bow down," and symbolizes our bowing down before the Lord in reverent worship, in spirit and in truth, and giving ourselves to God in total surrender. Worship means giving Him all the glory, all the honor, and all the thanksgiving. When I worship, it softens my heart and helps me to be able to hear God and to bless Him, and I can align myself to walk with Him and to receive the anointing. It is important that we invite significant discussion to the fourth ingredient, cassia, which points to worship in the life of the believer, because this is where strongholds are broken and yokes destroyed.

In this chapter, I want to move the theme from worship as dialogue to worship His presence. That is very graphically set forth in 2 Samuel 6, when David brings the ark of God into Jerusalem. The ark had long represented the presence of God with the people of Israel, but it had been lost to the Philistines. Upon David's defeat of the Philistines, he set his heart to transform the capital city of Jerusalem, which he had captured and made into his stronghold, into the national center of worship. To David, the ark meant the pure worship of God, and establishing it in his city would be a great national event for triumphant celebration.

However, because the priesthood had degenerated through the lax spiritual oversight of Eli, they disregarded God's specific instructions that the ark was to be carried by the sons of Kohath, not by a cart or any other vehicle (Exodus 25:14–15). The priestly rituals regarding the purpose of sacrifice and worship had gotten lost. In this instance, they tried to usher in the presence of God without abiding by the Word of God. Unfortunately, when the oxen stumbled en route, and it appeared that the ark was about to fall from the cart, a man named Uzzah took hold of the ark to steady it and in that tragic moment he died.

One can see why David wanted to bring the presence of God in the ark into Jerusalem, but a great price was paid because the presence of God and the anointing was treated the wrong way. The best of intentions are not good enough when it comes to the things of God. David was greatly upset about this, which motivated him to ask, "How do we usher in the presence?" They had to search in the Word of God to get clarity that the ark was to be borne on the shoulders of the priests.

To carry the ark of the Lord into Jerusalem was a twelve-mile uphill climb, and this time around, when they had only ventured six steps, David sacrificed oxen and fatted sheep (v. 13). He now understood that to bring the presence of the Lord to Jerusalem necessitated sacrifice and the shedding of blood. Some believe that David offered a sacrifice every six steps all the way there. In any case, David

It is important that we invite significant discussion to the fourth ingredient, cassia, which points to worship in the life of the believer, because this is where strongholds are broken and yokes destroyed.

made certain that it was a bloodstained path that represented the grace of God that paved the way for the presence of God. This reminds us not to take the anointing lightly, because it came at a precious cost.

In essence, this journey foreshadowed the bloodstained path that led Jesus from Jerusalem up to Calvary's hill. The blood that Jesus shed for us has made a way for us to go all the way into the presence of God. The enemy may say, "That's as far as you are going to go." But you can say, "No, I am going through because of Jesus' blood. Yes, I am going through the surgery. Yes, I'm going to start the business. Yes, I'm going through the rejection. Yes, I am going through the hurt and coming through victorious, because all the way along Jesus' blood has been shed."

David was so delighted about bringing the presence of the Lord into Jerusalem that he "danced before the LORD with all his might . . . with shouting and with the sound of the trumpet" (vv. 14–15). Those expressions of worship may not be in our liturgy, but they were in David's. He was dressed in a linen ephod, which was a fine garment, typically worn by the priests (Exodus 28:6), which doesn't mean he assumed a priestly role, but clearly he was leading his people to worship God's presence. He had a mighty praise that was going forth, and he danced so hard that his wife Michal despised him and accused him of "uncovering himself" as "one of the base fellows shamelessly uncovers himself" (v. 20). David responded sharply that he danced before the Lord's presence to celebrate God's goodness upon his life, and that he was not about to back off. The anointing on our lives may be misunderstood by others, and itself can become a source of criticism. The joy of His operative presence surpasses the disdaining comments of others.

Sometimes we have to come out of where we've been so we can put on the garment of praise and the oil of joy (Isaiah 61:3). We have to come out of what we designed and what we thought was suited for us. David found that the praise and the righteousness and the glory of God covered him. And, yes, it will cover you until you don't regard the things that are coming against you. It will cover you until the poison can't paralyze you. The fiery darts of the enemy can't pierce you.

It is a covering for you, and in worship we find another weapon. We are dancing out of old things. We are dancing out of tradition. We are going to take on a garment of praise and the oil of gladness. God has made a new place for us, a new *rhema* word for us, a new expression of faith for us, an anointing for where we are.

WHERE ADORATION AND WORSHIP LEAD US

While the elements of our worship are grounded in truth, the adoration is just an expression for how we love the Lord. We keep seeking to find more ways to express our passion for Him. Our love for and worship of God stretches our language to the upper limits. We start declaring that God is the greatest, greater than the greatest, bigger than the biggest, and higher than the highest, because we desire to communicate and dialogue with Him.

But our partner in the conversation is the transcendent God who is beyond, who hears us and speaks to us, whom we hear from and speak to, and there is a point at which we begin to adore the Lord until we feel as though our worship has somehow linked with another worship that is beyond ours, and we feel the help of angels. We sense that whatever the praise is in glory that we are somehow pulling in that frequency, and we begin to praise God in a sense of unity and oneness. That is what happens when we begin to adore God.

It is a place of sacred adoration of God. It is almost as though it peaks, and sometimes we find ourselves at a place of intimate silence. If you remember when the prophet Elijah met with the presence of the Lord on the mountain, the Lord was not in the wind, the earthquake, or the fire, but He was in "a still small voice" (1 Kings 19:11). The meaning of a *still small voice* is that God was in "the fine sound of silence." Sometimes we enter into that silent place in the presence of God where we do as Job did and lay our hand over our mouth and are utterly silent (Job 40:4). These are anointed moments of communication or worship in His presence.

Another register of worship is proclamation—the reading of the Word, the sharing of the Word, and the speaking of the Word. "The word of God is living and powerful, and sharper than any two-edged sword" (Hebrews 4:12). We don't just breeze over a scripture and say that we are worshiping the Lord, but we wait for the Word to "pierce even to the division of soul and spirit . . . to discern the thought and intents of the heart." It is to bring us to a place where the clichés that we use are exposed as empty shells, and we begin to try to give the highest quality of what we have to Him.

Thanksgiving is another register of worship. The chief ground of the dialogue of our conversation with the Lord is thanking God for His saving intervention when we were desperate and in need of rescue. Interventions are a popular method of behavior modification currently, but recall that God intervened or broke in on our reckless lives and rescued us from darkness to light. If it had not been for God intervening with His grace in our lives, we know what our ultimate end would be. Of course, we thank Him and begin to praise God. And so our thanksgiving becomes a confession of faith, because we believe that God has rescued us and counted us worthy as inheritors.

And then next, part of the register of our worship or a category of our expression to the Lord is commitment. We don't just glorify God and enjoy His presence and that's the end of it. No, we make a commitment. It is saying, "God, I trust You, and I am looking for Your mercy. I am asking and receiving forgiveness, and I am willing to forgive others." When we talk about commitment, it is confirmative. In other words, it is something that I must do, something that is transformative. There is no commitment if there is no performance of a commitment. So when we begin to worship God, we are brought to the place where our commitment is expressed in words such as, "I will trust in the Lord. I will commit my way to the Lord. I will give the sacrifice of praise. I will pay my vows before the congregation of the righteous" (Psalm 37). This speaks

The blood that Jesus shed for us has made a way for us to go all the way into the presence of God.

to a lasting fragrance emanating from our worship that culminates in committed actions.

Then our worship has petition and intercession. We intercede on the behalf of others. When go before the presence of God, we begin to move out of ourselves and begin to get the mind and heart of God and to pray for others. We develop a concern for others, and then God uses us. We call that "bridging the gap" ministry, when God uses us to stand in the gap for others and petition Him. We are called to be priests as intercessors before God, because we are part of the priesthood of all believers.

And then there comes a sense of expectation. That is still part of worship. We usually don't think of it as a different kind of prayer, but worship has all of this intermingled, and as we begin to intercede, we find that we are drawn from the present to anticipate and expect what God will do. We don't get up from praying or finish our worship without hope, but we are drawn toward a future. God has a plan for the future. God has good things ahead. He has a well-planned end ahead that we expect to see.

Have you discovered that? You start off heavy, weary, and burdened, but when you worship His presence and reflect on Him, He lifts you out of your old mindset and puts you in another place of praying for others who cannot pray for themselves. When you finish your petitioning, you are interceding, you are coming into a higher level of interaction with the presence of the Lord. And so this expectation causes us to look forward to what God is going to do next, and it gives us hope for a bright future.

THE CORPORATE ANOINTING

Just as there is an anointing for our individual lives, there is a corporate anointing for the body of Christ, His church. We are all parts of the body, whose head is Christ, "from whom the whole body, joined and knit together by what every joint supplies, according to the effective working by which every part does its share, causes growth of the body for the edifying of itself in love" (Ephesians 4:16). Each of us is a vital functioning part of the body, whether we serve as an eye or a foot, and each of us has an integral role in the church's growth through loving service.

In discussing the anointing for the corporate body of Christ with Pastor Rodney Derrick, who oversees the Professional Ministry Technicians at the Potter's House, he emphasized how important it is to help individuals find their place of anointed service within the body. Through the anointing, a person is enabled to carry out or operate in specific functions. Corporate anointing, authority, and power come from the cumulative personal anointings working in concert with one another (1 Corinthians 12–14). This is another instance of compounding of anointings.

However, some people will go into an area of service but don't have the grace or the anointing for it, and the consequences are never good. God created each of us a certain way, and to serve God's people takes both an anointing and a sacrifice. For instance, not everyone has the anointing to deal with people, which indicates that they are not equipped to serve as an usher or a counselor. You have to have the grace to help hurting people who are coming in from all walks of life and who are dealing with all sorts of issues and situations. There is training involved, sacrifice of time and energies, and gifts involved. The worst thing that a person can do is to try to step into a role to which they are not called.

Pastor Bonné Moon, who oversees the Potter's House School of Ministry, reinforced that it is paramount for every member of the body to have the anointing for what they do. How does one know whether they are in the right role? She stated that if what the person does is exhausting to them, they are probably not running in their anointed lane, because when you are in your lane, God just seems to give you the strength and joy to function there. The anointing brings with it a spiritual release that energizes; it is a gift of God's grace and a joy to serve others, not a service you must force yourself to do.

Once a person is in their anointed role, there are always challenges. There is always a process of growth in grace that can be very difficult. When things don't go well, some leave when it gets heated. Gold has to be refined, and we have to be willing to walk through the process. And as in all of life, there is a fine line with being the best that you can be in your service for God rather than trying to be better than the person who is serving next to you. The

THERE IS A POINT AT WHICH WE BEGIN

TO ADORE THE LORD UNTIL WE FEEL

AS THOUGH OUR WORSHIP HAS SOMEHOW

LINKED WITH ANOTHER WORSHIP

THAT IS BEYOND OURS, AND WE FEEL

THE HELP OF ANGELS.

reality is that Jesus' disciples were competitive, and so are we. The mother of James and John asked Jesus to grant her sons to sit on His right and left hand in His kingdom (Matthew 20:21), and we are not immune from the same selfish desires. The anointing only abides in humble places, both for us as individuals as well as for the corporate body.

In the broader picture, the corporate anointing is the presence of God. By that I mean that it is evident that the Holy Spirit is moving in our midst. When we corporately "set the LORD" before us and know that He is at our right hand (Psalm 16:8), we are cognizant that the anointing of the Holy Spirit is present. I like to think of it in the terms that the Holy Spirit takes over the place. "Now the Lord is the Spirit; and where the Spirit of the Lord is, there is liberty" (2 Corinthians 3:17). The working of the Spirit is evident by what we considered previously, that yokes are being broken from the necks "because of the anointing oil" (Isaiah 10:27). People will be delivered and set free from bondages that have enslaved them. When there is a crushing of the olive, and the oil begins to flow out over God's people, the church begins to grow in His presence. The yoke is destroyed because of the anointing, and there is liberty and great freedom. Even a small gathering of believers who are together in one place and acting together with singleness of purpose can generate a release of this power!

INGREDIENTS FOR THE CORPORATE ANOINTING

Deuteronomy 20 is an interesting text that has excellent applications to the concept of our corporate anointing. This chapter gives specific instructions to God's people when they were going to war together. When they were on the verge of battle, the priest was to declare to the people, "Hear, O Israel: Today you are on the verge of battle with your enemies. Do not let your heart faint, do not be afraid, and do not tremble or be terrified because of them; for the LORD your God is He who goes with you, to fight for you against your enemies, to save you" (vv. 3–4).

This speaks of the presence of God being with the gathered people of God, which is the anointing. It gives four specific instructions that tell us that when we go to battle, we need to be careful who goes with us. Specifically, it says to not take everyone into the fight. If there are some who are not operating in the corporate anointing, they are not to go with us. Rather, send them home to their families. Just as the anointing oil is only to include certain ingredients, certain elements were not to be a part of the battle.

Who is not to stay for the battle? First, there is the "man who has built a new house and has not dedicated it. Let him go and return to his house, lest he die in the battle and another man dedicate it" (v. 5). You can understand the division of this man's commitment. When it comes to our corporate anointing, this is talking about the house of our lives and of our hearts. If someone is not dedicated to the cause, if someone is not serious about what God has called us to be, they should go home with a divided heart and mind. Because when we are going into battle, we need to know that the people whom we are with are not mixed up about who God is, who heals us, who helps us, who saves us. You can't fight a battle with people who are mixed up about the house. We have to know that we are the temple of the Holy Spirit. We don't want people with us who have not yielded their hearts to the Lord. Otherwise, carnal minds and ideas will come in and captivate our minds and our hearts. We need a prayer life that will give us victory. There is protection, provision, and purpose that gets worked out and lived out in the united body.

The second criterion is, "Also what man is there who has planted a vineyard and has not eaten of it? Let him go and return to his house, lest he die in the battle and another man eat of it" (v. 6). This is saying that we have heard the Word and seeds have been planted in our lives, but have we partaken of

Just as there is an anointing for our individual lives, there is a corporate anointing for the body of Christ, His church.

it? In other words, the Word has been planted and given to us, but has it taken root? Do we have the spiritual fruit that should result from planting? I don't want to go to battle with someone who does not have love, joy, peace, longsuffering, kindness, goodness, faithfulness, gentleness, and self-control (Galatians 5:22–23). We do not want friendly fire to take us out of the battle. Friendly fire is never friendly and represents the house that is divided against itself that cannot stand. God gives us the triumph, but we must first be overcomers. We need to have a corporate anointing and stand together in unity.

The third point is, "And what man is there who is betrothed to a woman and has not married her? Let him go and return to his house, lest he die in the battle and another man marry her" (v. 7). This is saying that to be in the battle and win, we need to have people who understand the importance of covenant, because we are in covenant with God and with one another in the body of Christ. God is a covenant-keeping God with us, and we must be covenant keepers. We must be faithful to God and to His Word and be faithful to love and care for the members of His body. We need one another's gifts, wisdom, and power to be mutually edified.

And fourth, "What man is there who is fearful and fainthearted? Let him go and return to his house, lest the heart of his brethren faint like his heart" (v. 8). How difficult would it be to continue to pursue the battle when you see from inside the ranks there is reason to fear because of injuries inflicted by one another, i.e. expressive fear and unbelief. When one of us falls in the battle, it is disheartening. It is our responsibility to build one another up and never tear down. The Lord does not give us boldness in the Spirit to walk over and crush the faith of other believers. We are to have the bold love of Christ for others that makes coming to the Lord look attractive. The boldness is not that I can be more of me and who I am. The boldness is so I can be less of me and more like Christ. God wants us to do valiantly and stand for the presence of the Lord.

THE ANOINTING IS HIS PRESENCE

Just as God wants the anointing to be upon us as individuals, so He wants to anoint His whole body, the church. In a word, that anointing is knowing that the presence of God is with us, that Jesus Christ, the Anointed One, walks among us through the power of His Spirit. To truly be corporate, a fellowship of believers must surrender the tendency toward individuality and take on the mindset of an army going against an adversary. There is a corporate anointing and blessings that are poured out whenever the people of God assemble themselves and align themselves according to His Word. The beauty of it is that the anointing poured out on all of us is far greater than the anointing upon any one person or place! Together, we make up the fullness of His body!

It is our responsibility to build one another up and never tear down. The Lord does not give us boldness in the Spirit to walk over and crush the faith of other believers.

GOD WANTS TO LEAD YOU TO PLACES

YOU CANNOT GET TO WITHOUT HIM,

and He does that by the power of His Spirit.

HE CAN BRING YOU INTO THE REALM

OF THE MIRACULOUS—

God wants

NOT AS A SHOW,

but as a demonstration of His love

and compassion for the lost, hurting, or needy.

WHO AMONG US DOESN'T WANT

or need that?

STORMIE OMARTIAN

to lead you...

CHAPTER ELEVEN

TRANSFORMED

Now the Lord is the Spirit;

    and where the Spirit of the Lord is, there is liberty.

But we all, with unveiled face,

    beholding as in a mirror the glory of the Lord,

    are being transformed into the same image

    from glory to glory,

    just as by the Spirit of the Lord.

2 CORINTHIANS 3:17–18

e have seen that cassia, the fourth aromatic ingredient in the holy anointing oil (Exodus 30:22–25), was grown at high elevations where one has to climb up the mountain to find it, and that the etymology of the Hebrew word signifies "bowing the head in worship or great respect." We noted previously that within the anointing oil, cassia is proportionally the equivalent ingredient amount to the myrrh, which symbolizes suffering and troubles. That tells us that our worship should be proportionate to everything we've been through, and we have a praise that in quantity is tantamount and comparable to the difficulties and sufferings we've gone through.

When we worship the Lord, one of the things that happens is that our spiritual awareness of God is quickened. The more we talk about God, the better we visualize God. The more we meditate on God and who He is, the more we open our ears to hear God. In other words, we are spiritually awakened, and we get to a place where we know our God. As our focus is fine-tuned, we gain a deeper understanding of the attributes and nature of God. Spending time in His presence, we see not only the holiness of God, how separate and apart He is, but we see how beyond and above He is, how great and almighty He is.

As we worship, we find that our mind is fed. We are both nurtured and nourished. The apostle Paul said, "Let this mind be in you which was also in Christ Jesus" (Philippians 2:5). As we read His Word on our own and collectively with other believers, the Holy Spirit helps us and opens up the Word to our understanding. We are fed and carried along by the truth of God. Beyond that, as we worship the Lord, we also find that the wrong thoughts and imaginations that we should not entertain—thoughts of envy, doubt, disbelief, or fear—are cast down and purged, as well as the things that compete with the reality of Christ in our lives. Through it all, we find that we are "transformed by the renewing of our mind" that we "may prove what is that good and acceptable and perfect will of God" (Romans 12:2). A new and living way is indeed opened to us. This suggests that the anointing is essential not just for service but for the totality of our Christian vocation.

When we are in the presence of the Lord in worship, "the love of God" is "poured out in [our heart] by the Holy Spirit" (Romans 5:5), transforming our inner man, and we begin to love God in return and live as He would have us to live. And we love others because God has loved them, and they become loveable to us.

Worship is not just something we do once in a while during a church service, but it is part of our transformation through the anointing that God has given us. It is part of the Holy Spirit's means to changing us and making us who God has called us to be. As we worship the Lord whom we've come to love, we intentionally and joyfully take and devote our will to the purposes of God. Worship becomes the 24/7 whisperings of our heart to God and His whisperings back to us. It is the shouting of praise that comes from our inner man, and it is the declarations of God to us. It is an intimate place and a sacred space. It is a friendship, a walk, and a journey. It is a narrative, poetry, and prose. It is the embrace of God.

When we have tasted of the presence of God, life's pure river, once we know what it is to be in fellowship with Him, we long to be and live in His presence. We are seeking Him and searching for Him. We are saying, "Lord, where are You? I'm looking for You. I can't wait until I sense Your presence again." It is as though God breaks in on us, breaks in past all of the prison bars of our nature and our resistance and our self-righteousness. In His grace, Jesus comes in and visits and whispers and speaks peace to our soul.

And so our worship is simply our response to God's overtures and extensions of His love.

Some say that forms and rituals are a hindrance to real worship, but I disagree, unless they are made the focus rather than being the means to worship. We need wineskins to hold the wine, right? We need something with form, whether it's to raise our hands, to kneel, songs of worship, formal prayers, or Scripture readings according to a lectionary, to hold the contents of our worship. It's not about whether we stand or sit or have this custom or that custom. It is not about the form as long as it is accommodating to worshiping where God is in that moment. But we need forms that are accommodating to who and where we are. The main thing is that we know and enjoy the presence of the Lord.

WORSHIP BRINGS INNER TRANSFORMATION

A. W. Tozer said, "The essence of idolatry is the entertainment of thoughts about God that are unworthy of Him." It caused me to ask myself whether the thoughts that I think about God match the worthiness of God? Do I doubt that God can heal? Do I believe that some things are just impossible? Have I ceased to praise God for things that He has promised me but I've not yet received? Tozer's point is that because God is high, I must think high. Because God is lofty and lifted up, I must have a praise that exalts who God is. Anointed worship does more than help me to lift my hands, but I lift my heart and especially my thoughts.

When we worship, we want to ponder the Word of God and get to know the knowledge of God. We want to receive the thoughts and mind of God to a level where His Spirit teaches our spirit. That's where deep calls unto deep. That is when we sense that worship is more than what we can explain or talk about. That's when we have sensed somehow that we have connected with whatever the sound is in heaven.

And worship brings the inner transformation we so desperately need. God's presence brings us to a place where we want to confess what is wrong in our lives. When we become aware of the holiness of God, for instance, confession is naturally born in us. There is an openness, there is a revelation, and the more we see God, the more we see ourselves. The more we see the

Our worship is simply our response to God's overtures and extensions of His love.

grace of God, the more we see our weakness, our finiteness, and what we really deserve to receive. That's why in Isaiah 6, when the prophet saw the Lord sitting on a throne, high and lifted up and the glory filling the temple, he cried out, "Woe is me, for I am undone! Because I am a man of unclean lips, and I dwell in the midst of a people of unclean lips" (Isaiah 6:5). Here we find both an individual and a communal confession.

In the presence of God, our spontaneous response is the same as Isaiah's. We are fully exposed. That's why we don't have to pound away at people about what is wrong in their lives. If we are in the presence of the Lord and the living water is flowing in our midst, people are going to know their desperate need and reach out for His refreshing. When we come to pray with people, we don't have to say that this and that is wrong. If they get a glimpse of the glory of God, they will want the live coal from the altar of God that takes away their sin (v. 6). Whatever is flowing down from His presence, His fragrance and His aroma, is what they will want. Worship does all of that for us, plus helps to strengthen our belief.

Jesus said our highest priority is to "love the LORD your God with all your heart, with all your soul, with all your strength, and with all your mind" (Luke 10:27), and the anointing of God strengthens us to do that. The enemy will say to us, "You're never good enough. You'll never be able enough." But when we begin to worship God, we sense what God has said about us. When we see the manifest presence of God, and that His face has turned to us, and we are looking full into His wonderful face, we can say that we are strong enough to stand, to endure, and to go through as a good soldier. We can make it through the stress and the hard times with His anointing.

The anointing of God is essential. The fragrance of its spices on our garment keep coming as we stay in dialogue with God. We realize that "the veil of the temple was torn in two from top to bottom" (Matthew 27:51), and that through Jesus' death we have been given full access to "come boldly to the throne of grace" (Hebrews 4:16). The blood of the Lamb of God ushers us into the presence of the Lord, and in that place we are under the shadow of the Almighty. Under His wings we are in a place of safety, of protection, and of provision. In His presence, we have perpetual openness.

When we keep the worship channels open, our prayers are going up even while we are sleeping, and the Lord is sending blessings, sending help, dropping things our way. It is a freeway that doesn't shut down. It is an information highway that is never closed. In His presence, there are no traffic jams that keep us out. Every lane is a commuter lane, every lane is a fast lane, every lane is one that is open to you and me.

In worship, we walk with Him and live in Him, and it's only natural that we will be "singing and making melody in your heart to the Lord" (Ephesians 5:19). We find that there is a melody in our heart that never goes sharp or flat. There is a key that has been calibrated to the chorus of heaven. There are notes that have never been scored on a staff. There are rhythms that cannot be counted or numbered. There is something of the joy of the Holy Spirit that begins to stir in us, and heaven understands our song. Heaven knows our tune and our name, and when we begin to think of Jesus and begin to change keys and melodies, heaven knows our heart. Why? Because we have set our "mind on things above, not on things on the earth" (Colossians 3:2).

THE CORPORATE ANOINTING BRINGS US TRANSFORMATION

In the last chapter, we considered the place of corporate anointing and how worship takes us as a body to where we delight in the Lord and His presence. Hebrews 10:23–25 gives us additional instructions concerning the corporate anointing and how that brings us transformation: "Let us hold fast the confession of our hope without wavering, for He who promised is faithful. And let us consider one another in order to stir up love and good works, not forsaking the assembling of ourselves together, as is the manner of some, but exhorting one another, and so much the more as you see the Day approaching."

The writer is saying that the more we hold fast to our profession of faith, the more we live by faith, and the more we walk by faith and do not waver, we become aware that it isn't just us alone. It's about holding fast our professions of faith together as the body of Christ, and to do so we need to consider one another and how to stir one another up to love and good works. We come together in His Name to be a catalyst to one another, and we need one another. Together we sow, and together we reap the benefits. We provoke one another to grow, and we exhort one another that much more as we see the day of Jesus approaching. God has given us an open door to worship together as the saints of God in His presence.

There is a smorgasbord of God's goodness to partake of when we come together as the body of Christ, and particularly encouragement. Hebrews 10:35–36 states, "Therefore do not cast away your confidence, which has great reward. For you have need of endurance, so that after you have done the will of God, you may receive the promise." Keep the spirit of fervency together. Keep the fire lit. Keep the prayers going, and believe that God is for you and with you as the people of God. You will reap a harvest, but you have to confess it, believe it, and look for it together. No matter what the enemy says or does, the blessings of God are coming and overtaking you. Before you can open your mouths, before you can even call, God is answering. He is making a way.

Praise is your avenue to worship. Sometimes silence is your avenue to worship. Your liturgy of worship, whether it is singing, dancing, or praising the Lord, is your avenue of worship. We are talking about a place of worship and exhortation, a place where you can hear from the Lord. Not just for one but for the whole body, because He is present among you.

THE ANOINTING FOR ALL THAT WE NEED

In Mark 9:2–13, Jesus took Peter, James, and John, who were the inner circle of His disciples, up on a high mountain, where He was "transfigured

As we worship the Lord, we also find

that the wrong thoughts and imaginations

that we should not entertain—

thoughts of envy, doubt, disbelief, or fear—

are cast down and purged, as well as

the things that compete with the reality

of Christ in our lives.

before them." He was so full of the glory of God that His clothes became shining from the holiness within. As best we can understand this amazing meeting with Elijah and Moses, this was a discussion with Jesus that was preparing Him for what awaited Him in Jerusalem on His journey toward the cross. Peter was so overwhelmed that he broke in and suggested that they build tabernacles or booths for the three great personages, and they could spend more time together. But out of the overshadowing presence of God, the Father spoke and rebuked Peter, because in the presence of the Lord at that moment Peter's only role was to have obedient listening. Remember that we defined the anointing as the presence of the Lord.

The story continued as Jesus came down the mountain to where His other disciples and a great multitude gathered. It says, "Immediately, when they saw Him, all the people were greatly amazed, and running to Him, greeted Him" (v. 15). Let's presume that the people were so "amazed" because the clothes and the face of Jesus were still glowing from the glory of the transfiguration, similar to when Moses came down from the mountain after speaking with the Lord (Exodus 34:25). I assume that because, why else would they be "greatly amazed"?

In the crowd there was a father who said to Jesus, "Teacher, I brought You my son, who has a mute spirit. And wherever it seizes him, it throws him down; he foams at the mouth, gnashes his teeth, and becomes rigid. So I spoke to Your disciples, that they should cast it out, but they could not" (vv. 17–18). This man had a measure of faith, because he brought his son to Jesus, hoping that he would be delivered and healed. His statement is a reminder that people don't come to us or to our churches for us. They would be most miserable and greatly disappointed if that was the case. When they come into the body, they are looking for Jesus.

The Scripture indicates that the man's son was possessed by a very violent evil spirit that prevented him from speaking, and Jesus' disciples could not cast it out. *Could not* means that they didn't have the strength to do it. Jesus response, "O faithless generation, how long shall I be with you?" (v. 19), has the clear sense of frustration and irritation. Previously, Jesus had given the disciples the authority to cast out demons, and when they had been successful, they had boasted about how the demons were subject to them. Now they were unable to cast this spirit out. They had tried to do a new assignment that they had not been given the authority to do. Just because we have an anointing in one situation does not mean that we have that strength and empowerment for another situation. We must know in the body which assignment we have been given to do. When we step out of our anointing, we become an offense against the ministry and the body of Christ. Even more important, we may be anointed for a task, but due to a lack of faith, we fail to walk in that anointing or power.

So Jesus stepped in and said, "Bring him to Me," at which point the spirit saw Jesus and began to violently tear and afflict the boy in a horrific manner. Sometimes there is more violence and rage when it gets in the presence of the Lord. But you cannot assume that God is not going to answer just because it looks as though things are getting worse. In essence, the evil spirit was making a confession of who Jesus is. Demons recognized the person and power of Jesus even when the disciples did not, the father did not, the crowd did not, and the scribes did not.

Jesus asked the father, "How long has this been happening to him?" And the father responded, "From childhood." It was not that the child had done something wrong. Don't believe that because you are sick that there is sin. Sickness is a condition that entered the world through the sin of Adam and continues with our fallen humanity. Don't let the enemy condemn you because of a physical problem.

When Jesus asked the father about the symptoms, it was clear that the enemy had come to kill, steal,

When we see the manifest presence of God, and that His face has turned to us, and we are looking full into His wonderful face, we can say that we are strong enough to stand, to endure, and to go through as a good soldier.

and destroy the child. Sometimes the things that are raging in our lives are because the enemy is trying to destroy us. He is out to destroy our testimony, our faith, our love, and our hope. The enemy is raging because of the presence of Jesus, so do not fear.

The father pleaded to Jesus, "If You can do anything, have compassion on us and help us" (v. 22). He has faith, but not enough faith. How many times have we said, "God, if You can fix this! If You can hear me . . . if You can make it better!" We pray a faithless prayer. Interestingly, Jesus responded with an "If" of His own. "If *you* can believe, all things are possible to him who believes." He flipped it on the father, and on us. We want to make it a God problem when it's our problem. We are the ones who need to figure out the mind and the purpose of God. Even if our faith is small, it will suffice if it is anchored in the living Savior. I really believe that the words directed to the father were simultaneously directed to the disciples, who although they were called and anointed still labored with unbelief as the father did. It hampered the flow of their anointing.

God has given us an open door to worship together as the saints of God in His presence.

The father of the child cried out, not with tears but with sheer honesty and transparency, "Lord, I believe; help my unbelief!" (v. 24). He was saying, "I believe, but my belief has to grow. I have to believe to pray, and I have to pray to believe. I must believe to get in the presence of God and get in the face of God. I must get in the face of God so that my faith can be stronger."

Jesus then rebuked the evil spirit, and it came out. That which had rendered the boy unable to speak was gone. It makes me think about how hard the enemy tries to get believers to hold their tongues. He will do anything to keep us from speaking the Word of God as He has given it to us. I am so glad that we don't have to accept that spirit and that there is a living God who can speak to every fear and every doubt that holds us back. When Jesus sends forth His word of deliverance in our lives, it is as though the word ushers from the throne of God, travels all through the cosmos and down through time, and pierces our soul and accomplishes its work.

Please note that it wasn't the father alone who had unbelief. In privacy later, Jesus' disciples asked Him, "Why could we not cast it out?" (v. 28). Jesus could have exposed their own lack of faith publicly, but He took them aside in His kindness and answered, "This kind can come out by nothing but prayer and fasting."

I think Jesus was saying, "You thought there was just one kind of enemy, but he has all kinds of dimensions and levels. I want you to know that there are different levels of opposition. There are different levels of demons. There are different evil jurisdictions and spiritual hierarchies. There are principalities and rulers of wickedness in high places. You got excited because you had a few demons that were subject to you, and you felt so good that you wondered who was the greatest disciple in the kingdom. But when you ran into this *kind*, this granddaddy devil, he was not excited about your titles or claims. You can't just wish or hope this kind out. This kind of opposition is the kind that the doctor says is incurable. This type of opposition is when you're told it is impossible. This kind defies God in your life. This kind only comes out by prayer and fasting." Fasting is a self-inflicted myrrh in preparation for the anointing.

If you recall, after Jesus was baptized in the Jordan, the Father declared, "This is My beloved Son, in whom I am well pleased," and the Spirit of God descended like a dove and alighted upon Him (Matthew 3). Then "Jesus was led by the Spirit into the wilderness to be tempted by the devil," where He fasted and prayed and thoroughly defeated the enemy's lies and attacks (Matthew 4:1). Under the anointing and armed with God's Word, through prayer and fasting He overcame the enemy in the wilderness and finally "the devil left Him" (v. 11).

Joined by our faith in Jesus, under the anointing of His Spirit, we have the power over the enemy. We are not victims who must be subject to unbelief.

We have His anointing and access to God's presence. We can pray and get in the face of God and release our faith. We can live our best life and come through the battle victorious.

After Pentecost, the disciples and the apostles exercised the authority and power of Jesus over every power of the enemy. God didn't give us half of a prescription. He said that He has something for us that will equip us for everything that comes against us. He said that He has something that will keep us, something that will heal us, something that will lift us, something that will fill us, and something that will make us pure and sanctify us. The presence of God through the person of the Holy Spirit will answer our every need.

Together as the body of Christ, let us call upon God and gather in His Name. Let us be united in our faith and believe until every demon flees, until our sons and daughters are saved, until revival comes like a mighty wind. Let us pray until peace comes, until righteousness comes, until justice rolls. God can do it for all of us. Situations will shake up when we pray together. Prison doors will open up. Healing will come. When the corporate anointing flows and the people of God pray, power goes forth and joy is released. This is for the gathering of faithful believers who share the corporate anointing.

Just because we have an anointing in one situation does not mean that we have that strength and empowerment for another situation.

WITHOUT THE SPIRIT OF GOD

we can do nothing.

WE ARE AS SHIPS WITHOUT WIND

OR CHARIOTS WITHOUT STEEDS.

LIKE BRANCHES WITHOUT SAP,

we are withered.

We are as

LIKE COALS WITHOUT FIRE,

we are useless.

AS AN OFFERING WITHOUT THE

SACRIFICIAL FLAME,

we are unaccepted.

C. H. SPURGEON

hips without wind...

CHAPTER TWELVE

OVERCOMING POWER

"Not by might nor by power,

but by My Spirit,"

says the LORD of hosts.

ZECHARIAH 4:6

y now, you are aware of the ingredients in the holy anointing oil and what they symbolize—the myrrh for suffering and troubles, the sweet cinnamon for integrity, the calamus for uprightness, and the cassia for worship (Exodus 30:22–25). All of these were compounded and blended together with a hin of oil, which was pressed out of olives.

Blended together, we have seen that these ingredients represent the varied experiences in our lives, including the ones that we don't want to talk about. The ones that we hope no one ever finds out about. The ones that we wouldn't even want to put in a journal. And it includes all of the "not enough"s of our lives. Times when we haven't felt as though we prayed enough, sought God enough, or loved Him enough. God has taken all of those things, from the bests to the worsts, and worked them, and is working them, all out for the good.

Our God is not indifferent or complacent or absent. Our God will see us through. He will work with all the ingredients in our lives. He will take a divorce, the surgery, the separation from a friend, the failures, and the times of grief, and He will mix them into the compound. He will use the absence of a song and our heaviness. He will take the crushing and even bottle up the tears so they don't go to waste.

And what is He doing? He is creating a compound. He is mixing it together. He increases the anointing according to our needs. That is the economical move of God. You don't just suddenly show up and say, "Look, I'm anointed, and just last night I was gifted to teach. I've got a great gift to sing. I am anointed." No, it came. It was revealed. It was something in you as a child, and as you went along, it began to get opportunities for expression, and it was compounded. Anything that builds up gets momentum and impact. That's why Jesus could say, "And greater works than these he will do" (John 14:12). Greater works are possible because God has been building this up. He has been working it up in us so that He can use us.

The apostle Paul instructed Timothy "to stir up the gift of God" (2 Timothy 1:6). We need to stir up our gift as well. We need to stir up every gift and every calling that God has put in His people. It is compounded. People may ask you what God is doing in your life. Tell them He is compounding all of your life for His glory. He has been building you up.

It is the working of God that creates the anointing in our lives. He does it. It cannot be borrowed or imitated. It is not an adornment. It is not defined by educational degrees or denominational licenses. It is not a designer label or a class symbol. It is not connected to economic status. It is what causes us to believe that blind eyes and deaf ears can open. It's what empowers us to believe that jobs will come looking for us and that wayward sons and daughters can be saved. It's what we receive by being in the presence of the Lord.

"Give Me This Mountain"

I love the story of Caleb that is told in Joshua 14:6–14. Of the twelve spies whom Moses sent into the Promised Land, only Joshua and Caleb brought a report based upon the faith that they were "well able" to go in and conqueror the inhabitants. Because the two of them "wholly followed the Lord," God promised that the two of them would one day cross over into the land and receive their inheritance. Forty-five long years later, and at the age of eighty-five, Caleb is in the Promised Land and determined to receive his inheritance.

Caleb says to Joshua, "And now, behold, the Lord has kept me alive" (v. 10). He was saying, "Hey, I am still around. I didn't die without seeing

God's promise happen. It looks late. It looks delayed. It looks off schedule, but I am still alive to complete my destiny." And not only is he alive, but Caleb states, "As yet I am as strong this day as on the day that Moses sent me; just as my strength was then, so now is my strength for war, both for going out and for coming in" (v. 11). He was saying that if you want to know what kind of strength he still has, he may be eighty-five years old, but he has the strength to fight that he had when he was forty. He has the strength for war, and he's more than willing to enter the final conflict before settling down into comfort.

That is the anointing. Caleb knew what God had said to him, and he lived in the strength of the Word of God. He knew what God had put in his heart, and God had given him the strength for everything that He needed. It was, as the prophet Zechariah said, "'Not by might nor by power, but by My Spirit,' says the LORD of hosts" (Zechariah 4:6).

That is what I've said about the anointing—our spiritual man is always increasing in strength. It's not about going out to battle in our own strength. So in the presence of the Lord, our inner man should be waxing stronger day by day. And we do not have a right to move in comfort without anticipating and enduring conflict. We have the strength for war, both to go out and to come in.

What I really love is when Caleb looked Joshua in the eye and demanded, "Give me this mountain" (v. 12). That mountain, by the way, was still unconquered, had great and fortified cities, and it was said that the Anakim, or people of giant stature, were entrenched there—all of the reasons for why the people of Israel had failed to go into the land in the first place! He was saying, "Joshua, I've waited forty-five years for this day. God promised me this mountain. You don't have to help me fight for this. This mountain is mine."

God is taking all the ingredients of your life and strengthening you for whatever battles you face. You have the anointing, and you have the strength for war. Take every mountain that God has promised you!

"OVER ALL THE POWER OF THE ENEMY"

Joshua and Caleb and the people of God faced a host of enemies in the Promised Land, and so do you for yours. These were the people who did

God is taking all the ingredients of your life and strengthening you for whatever battles you face. You have the anointing, and you have the strength for war. Take every mountain that God has promised you!

not know the God of Israel. So many times we dismiss Old Testament names as though they are irrelevant, but the characteristics of the enemies that Israel faced are the same type of opposition that you and I face. And the names of the enemies reflected their opposition. My purpose here is to give you a glimpse at what they faced, and in doing so, what we face as well in spiritual battle.

Israel was going into Canaan, and one of their enemies was the *Canaanites*, which means "to press down or to humiliate." Whenever God has given us an assignment or a purpose in our lives, we confront that which opposes that purpose. To press down or humiliate, the enemy will use sickness or poverty or whatever happens to bring us down. The enemy will bring circumstances that press us to spend a great deal of our time dealing with them. The challenge for us is to not allow situations and circumstances to hold us down.

As believers, we are called to live above and beyond our circumstances. "Come what may," we need to say, "I am going to serve God. With or without the job, I'm going to give God praise. Healthy or not, I am going worship. Loved or rejected, I will serve the Lord faithfully." And so the anointing of God gives us the victory to rise above circumstances, because God's Word is our highest reality. We do not depend on what we see, hear, or feel, but what God has said. It's the highest form of our reality. And that reality will bring joy and peace to us as we believe.

"Why are you cast down, O my soul? And why are you disquieted within me?" (Psalm 43:5). We look at our circumstance and say, "Why am I feeling depressed? Why am I dealing with this? Why am I humiliated? Why am I held down and pressed down? Why is there resistance?" We counter that with the psalmist's answer: "Hope in God; for I shall yet praise Him, the help of my countenance and my God."

The people of God also faced the *Hittites*, which is a word that means "fear or terror." So many of the children of God have missed their promised land because they gave in to fear, worry, and anxiety. Fear, if we allow it to take root, will tear our faith and hinder the anointing. Not surprisingly, in the Bible we have no less than three hundred and sixty-five times where the Word of God says, "Do not fear." It is a divine prescription for every day of the year. The Lord has said, "I will never leave you nor forsake you" (Hebrews 13:5). He is going to protect us against any enemy that we encounter on this journey.

Another group that Israel confronted to get to their promise was the *Perizzites*, which means "an unwalled city." These are people who have no boundaries or set limits in their lives. They are totally insecure, up one day and down the next. This spirit is the one that challenges us and wants us to have a complete lack of discipline and consistency in our lives. Here's a biblical description of them: "Whoever has no rule over his own spirit is like a city broken down, without walls" (Proverbs 25:28). We are to have a spirit that is disciplined and submitted to the rule of the Word of God. Sometimes I hear someone say, "I am committed to Jesus," but it is obvious from their lifestyle that they are not "committed" enough to be committed to discipline. To abide in the anointing involves the discipline to pray, to seek God, to be in Bible study, to worship, to share the Good News with others, and, yes, to clean our homes. I do not mean the discipline of legalism or trying to win God's favor, but if we organize our life around the things of God, we will see the anointing flowing and discipline will be part of a walk by faith through grace.

"NOTHING SHALL BY ANY MEANS HURT YOU"

The list of enemies is lengthy. There were also the people called the *Amorites*, which means "to speak or say" and implies negative speech. It is characterized by criticism and complaining, particularly self-pity. It cries, "I am feeling

To abide in the anointing involves

the discipline to pray, to seek God,

to be in Bible study, to worship,

the share the Good News with others,

and, yes, to clean our homes.

bad. Nothing ever works out for me. Everyone is against me. Why must I do this? Why do I have to go through this?" It is the murmuring, the complaining, and the disputing that are not to be a part of our lives (Philippians 2:14). It was precisely the spirit that prevented the people of Israel from going immediately into the Promised Land. It is so easy to be discouraging and to throw ice water on others with our words. So we ask the Lord to "set a guard, O LORD, over my mouth; keep watch over the door of my lips" (Psalm 141:3). The Bible tells us that we should discipline our minds: "Whatever things are true, whatever things are noble, whatever things are just, whatever things are pure, whatever things are lovely, whatever things are of good report, if there is any virtue and if there is anything praiseworthy—meditate on these things" (Philippians 4:8). The answer to negativity and complaining is to have a grateful heart. "Rejoice always, pray without ceasing, in everything give thanks; for this is the will of God in Christ Jesus for you" (1 Thessalonians 5:16–18).

Jebusites means "to trample." This is very close to the meaning of *Canaanites*, which actually is closer to oppression while this is closer to depression. Now today you may be in a good space, but all of a sudden you feel a heaviness come over you, and you wonder where it came from. The enemy will try to keep us in this trampled over place. The Word of God says that He has given us "the oil of joy for mourning, the garment of praise for the spirit of heaviness" (Isaiah 61:3). God has woven an anointed mantle for us. He has secured a pathway for us to get out of heaviness. I am not talking about being somber or serious. I am talking about being weighed down in the dumps. We may go there, but we don't stay there. Psalm 68:2 says, "As wax melts before fire," so the heaviness is melted by the presence of the Lord.

The word *Midianites* means "strife and contention." This is precisely what will paralyze our covenant relationships. It will hinder family relationships, marital relationships, working relationships, and ministry relationships. We cannot continue when we have strife and disagreements. This is why Psalm 133 tells us "how good and how pleasant it is for brethren to dwell together in unity!" and compares it to the precious anointing oil running down on Aaron's beard.

When the ungodly people were building the tower of Babel (Genesis 11), the Lord said about them, "Indeed the people are one and they all have one language, and this is what they begin to do; now nothing that they propose to do will be withheld from them" (v. 6). If a wicked people can get together for what opposes the purpose of God, I know the chosen people of God can get together for the glory of God.

Among the body of Christ today, we have different perspectives on issues, but we should commit to being disciplined toward building one another up. "Only let your conduct be worthy of the gospel of Christ, . . . stand fast in one spirit, with one mind striving together for the faith of the gospel" (Philippians 1:27). We commit to the power that comes from our common agreement in the gospel. We commit to bringing our individual anointings together in a humble manner that leads to a corporate anointing. As the Spirit of God is lifting a brother or sister, we get lifted higher in our spirit. We feed off of one another. We can't wait to boast and brag about what God is doing in another member's life. That is how the anointing oil flows and the lantern captures the oil and creates the light.

Another people group, the Philistines were almost a universal problem to the people of God. *Philistine* means "to wallow in the dust," which surely is a spirit of self-pity. It is where one gives too much deference to the flesh rather than to the truth of what God has stated is true about us. It is a selfish attitude rooted in haunting lies, which must be driven out and kept out by fully embracing and declaring what the Word of God says about us.

Moabites simply means "against." It represents a spirit of rebellion or lawlessness. It is a similar to an unwalled city or having no rules for our lives. It leads to living in a dry parched place without the refreshing of God.

"Until They Are Destroyed"

"And the LORD your God will drive out those nations before you little by little; you will be unable to destroy them at once, lest the beasts of the field become too numerous for you. But the LORD your God will deliver them over to you, and will inflict defeat upon them until they are destroyed" (Deuteronomy 7:22–23). Sometimes it is a gradual work to see the enemy driven out. In other words, it might be a process, and one that does not happen overnight. But we have the certainty that ultimately they will be defeated.

Why the process? The Lord said that if it happens too fast, the beasts would become too numerous. I'm not certain what He means, but I think it means that as we grow and develop and mature in the things of God, the process of fighting the enemy keeps us praying, keeps us seeking God, keeps us needing God. We recognize that in the process God is working everything for my good, even the enemy's opposition. We can thank Him for the hard times. We can thank Him for heaviness that we have to push through. We can praise Him for the discipline and rules that are being built into our lives.

I am reminded of the story of Esther, who was orphaned as a child and adopted by her godly cousin Mordecai while living among the Jewish exiles in Persia. She was a beautiful lady who submitted herself to Mordecai's teachings and wisdom. After Esther was chosen as one of the many candidates to become the wife of King Ahasuerus, it states: "Each young woman's turn came to go in to King Ahasuerus after she had completed twelve months' preparation, according to the regulations for the women, for thus were the days of their preparation apportioned: *six months with oil of myrrh*, and six months with perfumes and preparations for beautifying women" (Esther 2:12).

Esther spent six months of going through this spicing and cleansing with the oil of the bitter myrrh, and then another six months in other sweet spices. That was similar to the anointing oil. There is another prescription that is called the sacred oil. Esther purifies herself and represents the anointing oil of the Spirit. She represents the Spirit-filled

We commit to bringing our individual anointings together in a humble manner that leads to a corporate anointing.

church as the bride of Christ. That is the overcoming church that reflects the beauty and the fragrance of the Lord Jesus Christ.

We see how the Lord used Esther to be the rescuer for His people. He gave her plans and strategies and designs to counter the enemy's attack, and she submitted herself to God's will even unto the possibility of death, accepting the fact that it was for this time she had come into the kingdom.

I want you to consider that you may be the key person to making the changes that make a difference in your family, your neighborhood, your job, or your church. Don't assume that it is necessarily the person who is in charge. You may be the one who captures the vision in the body of Christ and is able to advance the cause in unique ways. Don't underestimate the move of the anointing upon your life.

"BY HIS SPIRIT!"

Before I close, I want to review Exodus 30:22–25: "Moreover the LORD spoke to Moses, saying: 'Also take for yourself quality spices—five hundred shekels of liquid myrrh, half as much sweet-smelling cinnamon (two hundred and fifty shekels), two hundred and fifty shekels of sweet-smelling cane [calamus], five hundred shekels of cassia, according to the shekel of the sanctuary, and a hin of olive oil. And you shall make from these a holy anointing oil.'"

The first spice is myrrh, which means "bitterness," and is bitter to the taste. It is symbolic of the things that I want to avoid, the painful and distasteful experiences of life. However, they have a great value, because they produce a pleasing fragrance. Myrrh was one of the three gifts brought to the baby Jesus by the wise men. Some have said that myrrh represented one of the three offices that Jesus walked in, the office of the prophet, which often involved the speaking of truth with power and was bitter when the listeners refused to receive it. Jesus was called the Man of sorrows both in life and death. To the believer, myrrh symbolizes a life of true discipleship to the Lord. Jesus put it in these terms: "Whoever of you does not forsake all that he has cannot be My disciple" (Luke 14:33).

Sweet cinnamon, the second spice of the anointing oil, comes from the bark of a tree and has a sweet fragrance. The root of the word *cinnamon* means "erect, to stand straight." It represents integrity and walking in truth. The cinnamon flower's smell is offensive, but the bark is sweet, which represents God's people living in the midst of a corrupt society and yet in an abiding relationship with the Lord. The apostle Paul says, "Do all things without complaining and disputing, that you may become blameless and harmless, children of God without fault in the midst of a crooked and perverse generation, among whom you shine as lights in the world, holding fast the word of life, so that I may rejoice in the day of Christ that I have not run in vain or labored in vain" (Philippians 2:14–16).

Calamus, or sweet cane, is the third ingredient, a tall weed that grows in a hostile environment. The word literally means "branch or weed." Calamus speaks of that living, abiding relationship between the vine and the branches (John 15). It is a rod of strength through which the oil can flow as a channel. We live in a hostile environment that makes it impossible to produce fruit unless we abide in a relationship with Jesus. But if we do maintain that relationship, nothing in this environment can keep us from bearing fruit. Our God has said, "Because he has set his love upon Me, therefore I will deliver him. I will set him on high, because he has known My name" (Psalm 91:14).

The fourth ingredient of the holy anointing oil, cassia, is found in the bark of a tree that grows in high altitudes and possesses a little purple flower. Biblically, the word means "bowing down and chivalry." It speaks of bowing down before the Lord in reverent worship and giving ourselves to God in total surrender. Giving Him all the glory, giving Him all the honor, and giving Him all the thanksgiving. Cassia means that we must worship the Lord "in spirit and in truth" (John 4:24). When I worship, it softens my heart and helps me to be able to hear God and to bless Him and walk with Him. Through worship, we "enter into His gates with thanksgiving, and into His courts with praise. Be thankful to Him, and bless His name" (Psalm 100:4).

Olive oil, free flowing olive oil, is the ingredient that binds all of the spices together. This blending together of sweet and bitter speaks of the unity involved. This is the unity of Psalm 133: "Behold, how good and how pleasant it is for brethren to dwell together in unity! It is like the precious oil upon the head, running down on the beard, the beard of Aaron, running down on the edge of his garments. It is like the dew of Hermon, descending

You may be the key person to making the changes that make a difference in your family, your neighborhood, your job, or your church. Don't underestimate the move of the anointing upon your life.

upon the mountains of Zion; for there the Lord commanded the blessing—life forevermore." Scripture calls us to come into the unity of the Spirit. It calls us to come and to grow into the stature of the fullness of Christ.

Under the anointing, "We know that all things work together for good to those who love God, to those who are the called according to His purpose" (Romans 8:28). Under the anointing, "What then shall we say to these things? If God is for us, who can be against us? He who did not spare His own Son, but delivered Him up for us all, how shall He not with Him also freely give us all things? Who shall bring a charge against God's elect? It is God who justifies. Who is he who condemns? It is Christ who died, and furthermore is also risen, who is even at the right hand of God, who also makes intercession for us. Who shall separate us from the love of Christ? Shall tribulation, or distress, or persecution, or famine, or nakedness, or peril, or sword? As it is written: 'For Your sake we are killed all day long; we are accounted as sheep for the slaughter.' Yet in all these things we are more than conquerors through Him who loved us" (vv. 31–37).

As the myrrh and the cinnamon and the calamus and the cassia work together for our good, "I am persuaded that neither death nor life, nor angels nor principalities nor powers, nor things present nor things to come, nor height nor depth, nor any other created thing, shall be able to separate us from the love of God which is in Christ Jesus our Lord" (vv. 38–39). Everything that came and everything that departed is working together for our good because He is Lord.

In the presence of God, we are reminded that we cannot give up, that we have not been forgotten. Under the anointing, we are reminded that it is not more that we can bear, that the temptation will not overtake us. We know what God promised, what He has said, that strengthen us for the battle. We are able because it is not by our might or power but by His Spirit, thus says the Lord.

"So, Jesus, the Anointed One, I surrender absolutely to your Lordship. I ask for and receive Your anointing. I receive my healing and deliverance. I can put the rebellious things out of my life, those things that bind me. Under the anointing, I will walk through the tribulation, the persecutions, the trouble, and the hardships and come out on the other side. 'If the Son makes you free, you shall be free indeed' (John 8:36), and I want to be free. Everything that would rise up and exalt itself against the Name and the power and the presence of Jesus Christ has to go. Because of the shed blood of Jesus, there is liberty, there is peace, there is freedom, there is joy, there is help, and there is hope. Amen."

We know what God promised, what He has said, that strengthen us for the battle. We are able because it is not by our might or power but by His Spirit, thus says the Lord.

BIBLIOGRAPHY

BOOKS:

Hagin, Kenneth. *Understanding the Anointing.* Oklahoma: Rhema Bible Church, 1982

Hinn, Benny. *The Anointing.* Nashville: Thomas Nelson Publishers, 1997

Jakes, T. D. *Anointing Fall on Me*, Maryland: Pneuma Life, 1997

Nee, Watchman. *The Release of the Spirit.* Indiana: Sure Foundation, 1964

Wilke, Lori. *The Costly Anointing.* Destiny Image, 1991

ARTICLE:

Lee, Witness. *The Church—The Reprint of the Spirit.* Anaheim Living Stream Ministry, 1987